Contents

Contents

1

Setting the scene

For some thirty years organizations have been developing computer-based information systems and before this people, paper, pens, calculators and mechanical punch card machines were the main tools available for data manipulation. These tools and even the early computers were awkward to use and much effort was expended in ensuring they were utilized efficiently and correctly. However, over the last thirty years the technology has been developing very quickly and hence new problems associated with its use have tended to appear with alarming frequency. It was fruitless to focus upon the potential offered by this developing technology until the technical problems of its operation were more or less stabilized. The tasks undertaken by the early computer equipment were those which were the most obvious to identify and the easiest for the computer to improve, such as accounting, invoicing, and other labour intensive data-based office activities of the 1950s and 1960s. This is not meant as a criticism of the early developers of information systems – it would have been disastrous to apply the early computer technology to anything more sophisticated until it was better understood and proven.

The vast majority of the issues addressed throughout the 1960s, 1970s and even the early 1980s were issues associated with how to 'supply' information systems to business. As the supply issues have become better understood, and with many of the basic systems of organizations having been automated, attention has turned to more imaginative and fruitful applications of the technology. This shift of attention has highlighted new issues associated with ascertaining 'demand' for information systems in organizations. No longer are organizations content to focus upon the obvious – they are now searching for new opportunities. The mid-1980s saw the development of several techniques to help analyze an organization's objectives and methods of operation in order to reveal more innovative opportunities based on information systems. This focus on ascertaining demand has not detracted from issues of supply, but rather has broadened the range of matters to be considered. The focus of the late 1980s was upon the importance of determining demand, often driven by the need to use information systems to gain competitive advantage for business, or at least to avoid being disadvantaged.

Supply issues are very much the province of information technology managers and specialists – often the people who have developed with the technology during the 1960s and 1970s. In this book supply issues will be referred to as information technology (IT) issues. Compare the IT people with those that are able to analyze the business using an intimate knowledge of the business process to reveal opportunities. Usually such knowledge is accumulated by management and functional specialists and can be applied by them in deciding what the organization needs in terms of information systems. Ascertaining demand is a management task and the issues concerned will be referred to in this book as information systems (IS) issues. The phrases IS and IT cannot be used to have exclusive and distinctive definitions because some of the issues associated with matching supply and demand overlap. However, some distinction needs to be made between supply and demand issues – Figure 1.1 summarizes the differences.

Both IS and IT have 'strategic' and 'tactical' components. By strategic we mean those issues of a longer term nature which require to be addressed by senior management infrequently. By tactical we mean those issues of an operational short-term nature which are generally the concern of middle management and specialists. Strategy concerns creating a vision of the future and the means and policies which will enable the organization to reach that vision, whereas

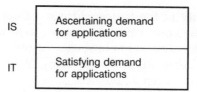

| IS | Ascertaining demand for applications |
| IT | Satisfying demand for applications |

Figure 1.1 Prime issues

2

tactical matters are concerned with applying the rules and making things happen. Clearly these descriptions are very general and more precise definitions will be presented as the book progresses.

Figure 1.2 relates the strategic and tactical notions to the earlier discussion of IS and IT. The contents of the four quadrants show the basic issues of concern to each box. For example, the board members of every large organization need to ensure that the general managers of each of the areas of business within the organization consider how applications of information technology can enhance that business and possibly underpin the competitive position of the business unit. This is a strategic IS issue which can be accomplished in a variety of ways, for example by insisting that such matters are discussed in the business plans submitted to the board members. Turning to tactical IS, business unit managers need to ascertain the systems required to operate in their business unit and to rank the importance of these to provide direction for the suppliers of these systems. This can be achieved in a variety of ways by the business, but in practice it is often delegated to consultants. For strategic IT the supply of applications can be managed in many ways. For example, it may be possible to supply every person in the organization with a personal computer and allow every application to be developed separately, or an alternative would be a centralized supply strategy with systems supply always coming from a central unit with operation on a centrally located machine. This issue is a strategic IT matter requiring rules to be formulated long before supply commences. The last of the four boxes concerns tactical IT issues. This box contains all the

	Strategic	Tactical
IS	Creating an environment to enable demand to be related to business strategy	Ascertaining the applications required for the business
IT	Creating the managerial and technical environment in which supply is to take place	Managing resources and supplying the business with applications and technology

Figure 1.2 Management issues

detailed issues of acquiring and using a particular application, for example, the specification of detailed security requirements.

Very senior managers or possibly corporate board members need to be concerned with strategic IS. Tactical IS is the province of managers of particular business units. Strategic IT is an issue to be addressed jointly by senior management/corporate board members and senior IT managers. Tactical IT is an issue to be addressed jointly by IT staff, managers of particular business units and managers working at a functional level within the business unit. Observation of the real world would suggest that this is not always understood by those concerned and often is not undertaken by those managers specified. Frequently the IT management is charged with most of these duties but when attempting to discharge them has little success and is then blamed for systems that do not meet business requirements. Figure 1.3 summarizes the appropriate management to deal with each of the four areas.

This book considers all four issues, focusing upon the management issues in each box. The technical aspect of, for example, selecting the appropriate programming language for an application (a tactical IT issue), is excluded as this is not a concern of the intended readership of this book.

Chapter 2 is concerned with various ways of classifying IS and IT to demonstrate the breadth of the subject and the types of information system addressed by the book. Chapter 3 raises some of the management issues involved as, historically, the subject has been the province of the technician and without some clarification our focus could cause problems for some readers. Interestingly, many of the problems of the subject are assumed to be technical inadequacies when in reality they occur because of insufficient or inadequate management activity. The following four chapters (4, 5, 6 and 7)

	Strategic	Tactical
IS	Corporate board members	Business unit managers
IT	Corporate board members/senior IT managers	IT staff/business unit managers/ functional level management

Figure 1.3 Management concerned

4

consider the issues of strategic IS, tactical IS, strategic IT and tactical IT respectively. Chapter 8 brings the issues together and Chapter 9 considers the future impact of IS upon our society and considers the medical, privacy, organizational and employment issues raised by widespread use of the technology.

This book is not for 'dipping into'. It begins by introducing ideas and a simple vocabulary that is extended as the book progresses, so to read, say, chapter 8 in isolation would be non-productive. It would be the delight of the authors to provide definitive answers to all the issues raised but, alas, such answers are not readily available as yet. We are dealing with a very young discipline with a history of scarcely more than thirty years. If the reader is looking for the certainty of subjects such as accountancy he or she will be disappointed.

The benefits to be gained from studying this book will vary depending upon the focus and organizational level of the reader. However, the benefits outlined below will apply to all the parties involved in the IS/IT process. The book will provide an understanding of the framework in which activities of the individual parties should take place. Readers should be able to appreciate where their particular activity is required and also where it is not required: or it could prevent normal managers becoming born-again IT experts! Additionally the book will provide an overview of the tools required to ascertain the 'demand' for a business and the alternative methods of supply. Finally, it will assist senior managers in expressing their requirements to more junior staff.

Therefore, we can state very clearly what this book will not do – it will not assist you in understanding the technical issues of computing. If you were not able to compare the relative benefits of Ethernet vs. Twisted pair as means of local area networking before you read this book, you will not be in a position to undertake it at the end. Throughout the book we intend to take a management perspective.

2

What are information systems?

With a discipline as young as information systems, definitions of what is included and what is excluded are difficult. As a means of portraying boundaries we will describe a day in the life of a marketing executive working for an international games producer. First the events in the day will be explained and then a number of classifications will be analyzed drawing upon the earlier discussion for examples.

John is awakened at six-thirty a.m. as usual to hear the morning business news – the dollar has fallen yet again. While shaving he wonders how those US sales targets will ever be reached. Still, that problem is for later; first he must fight the crowds on British Rail – today he might even get a seat! Arriving at the station John meets Peter York who is the general manager responsible for UK production. After the usual moans about British Rail, John learns of major sourcing difficulties with plastic playing pieces from their Hong Kong subcontractor. John remembers thinking this could happen, but was assured the matter was under control. The new products will probably not be ready for delivery which will not please the customers. No doubt he will be told of the problem formally in due course.

British Rail must be having a good day because he is early to the office and is greeted by Gill, his super-efficient secretary. He notes the morning mail, especially a note from the public relations agency which will require urgent action. He scribbles his comments on the letter and sends it to the chief executive. The telephone book tells him of ten calls still awaiting reply. Possibly more importantly Gill tells him of the dissatisfaction in the sales office with at least five of the clerks talking of looking for new jobs. Still all that can wait a while.

Turning to his newly installed personal computer he logs-on to the electronic mail system to find he has fifteen new messages awaiting reading. He is amazed how this new form of communication has grown over the last two years – nearly everyone in the company is now on the system. He scans the titles of the messages and finds that at least half are copies of reports sent to other people in his department and have been copied to him for his information. This seems to be happening more these days with the new technology. At least the document he really wants is there, which is the periodic international sales report. He reads this very carefully and attempts to draw conclusions from the mass of statistics presented. He notes the compiler has attempted to draw just such conclusions but he always prefers his own interpretation rather than that of others he has not even met. Moving on he notes a request for a meeting from his manager which is hardly a real 'request' but more a summons! He notes this in his pocket diary and tells Gill to put it in the desk diary.

So to the first meeting of the day which is a discussion of the arrangements for a new product launch. John thinks these meetings drag on because the chairman does not control the attendees – John makes a mental note to arrange a showing of the John Cleese video on meetings. However, this is unlikely to happen because his mental notes have a habit of creating little action. Arriving back at the office he telephones a product manager to ask for more information on the item under discussion at the meeting. He is surprised to learn that the product is unlikely to be available on time and hence the whole meeting was rather pointless. However, he will need the information for the following season's launch so he tells the subordinate to produce the analysis anyway.

The detail of the international sales report arrives, this time on paper, so John takes out the vital statistics and prepares a management commentary for the directors which he then gives to Gill to action on her word processor. He tells Gill to telefax it to the director upon completion of the typing.

On leaving the office for lunch he notices Gill dealing with a large pile of documents – she tells him that these are new staff slips, one per employee, being processed for a secretary in an adjoining office who is particularly busy. The lunch is with a long-standing and loyal customer who inadvertently tells John of a major promotion for a new range of products being proposed by a competitor. On returning to the office John sends an electronic mail message to all his product managers reporting this gem of information.

Then it is back to boredom – authorizing salesmen's bonuses. He wonders why he has to do this every month as he seldom changes anything. As a break he enters the information gained at lunch into the competitor database, wondering all the time if he is the only person to update this database. Then, more bonuses to authorize punctuated only by a break to access an external database held by a trade association to which the company belongs. There is no indication at all on this database that the competitor mentioned at lunch is contemplating an expansion of the product range.

For another break he wanders off to see Jim Wallace, a friend who runs the data processing department. Discussions of football and the tribulations of Luton Town lead Jim to explain how busy his department is. Apparently the number of invoices produced in the last week exceeded the previous maximum. John knows that this does not necessarily mean a higher sales volume in the next month's statistics but it is a positive sign. John has a cup of coffee and then returns to his office for the next meeting.

John had been looking forward to this meeting all week because the system under discussion will ease his life considerably. Linking his company's computer with that of his major customers has been in operation for two years, but the new proposal is to extend this to allow customers to see the company's stock levels and vice versa. John will support the matter in any way he can. The meeting ends with a firm timetable for implementation, but John wonders whether the consultancy will deliver the software on time.

John then starts his journey home after another tiring day. He checks the electronic mail on his portable – just more junk mail and copies of other people's letters sent for information. Another day ends as it began with the nine p.m. news reporting that the dollar is down again.

The foregoing description of John's day focused upon his receipt, despatch and processing of information because this aspect is the focus of this book. However, even if we took a more balanced view of John's day it would still show that information processing is a central feature of the process of managing.

The first important classification to mention is the difference between informal and formal information systems. The information gleaned on the train, that received from Gill regarding low motivation levels in the sales department and that vital piece of information received at lunch were not the result of a design process. It could be said that they occurred by accident, for example nobody designed the fact that Peter York caught the same train as John. Compare this with the international sales report which clearly arrived as a result of some

	Formal	Informal
Non-routine	Database integration systems can assist here	Can IT provide the infrastructure for this to occur? For example, electronic mail systems
Routine	Ripe for automation!	Be aware when designing the formal. Some of this may be able to be incorporated

Figure 2.1 Mapping by formality and routine

design process. However, the matter may not be as clear as this – it could be that the lunchtime entertaining of the customer was designed for just the outcome described, namely the collection of information. Some organizations try to formalize the informal – the American tradition of the Friday 'beer-bash' when people stop work early to drink beer and meet other organizational members is an example of formalizing the informal. The important point is that this book is focusing on designed (formal) information systems and not the informal. However, sight must never be lost of the existence of the informal and the superb way in which it can operate. Sometimes rumours can spread faster than paperwork can carry the true facts!

Associated with the formal/informal classification is the notion of routine and non-routine information. Routine implies that the information is produced to some timetable, for example the periodic international sales report. However, the type of information produced as it is required and which may not even be produced again is non-routine information. John's inputting the data to the competitor database is an example of a non-routine activity. Mapping formal/informal with routine/non-routine provides Figure 2.1. Routine/formal activity is ripe for automation, whereas the non-routine/informal activity is nearly impossible to plan and hence generic systems like electronic mail are the limit of the activity. Interestingly routine/formal information is usually associated with junior and middle management whereas non-routine/informal is associated with senior management.

A second important classification is that between manual systems, for example the hand written comments on public relations' letter, and computer-based systems, for example the electronic mail system. This book focuses primarily upon computer-based systems, but the tools of analysis to be presented are valid equally for manual systems,

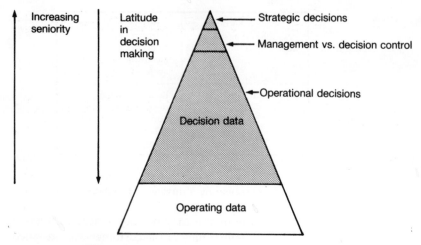

Figure 2.2 Mapping by level of decision making

although a little over-complex for such simple systems. Interestingly many of the electromechanical systems used in organizations are being replaced by computer-based systems, for example telephone switchboards are now largely computer driven and hence the data generated are available for further analysis.

During John's day he received volumes of information from other organization members which he summarized and passed upwards in the hierarchy. This is a very typical management practice. Figure 2.2 illustrates this process by dividing the decisions made by managements into three types. The first type, often called *strategic decisions*, relates to those long range, complex and unstructured decisions said to be made by senior management. Information for such decisions is often ill defined, required on a non-recurrent basis, originates from sources external to the organization, gathered in an informal way, and highly summarized. Systems to supply such information to senior management are known as 'executive information systems'. John adding his piece of gossip gained at the lunch table is a way of formalizing what in the past may have been lost information.

The second type of decisions illustrated in Figure 2.2 are often called *management control decisions* and are taken by middle managers. These often result from comparing some information to a standard or budget and any difference forces the consideration of alternative courses of action. Information for such decisions is often internally focused, short term, historical, relatively easily predefinable, and required on a routine basis. John was dealing with such information when he examined the periodic international sales report. He could have been looking at the report with certain expectations in mind and he was in fact looking for variations from his expectations.

The third type of decisions illustrated in Figure 2.2 are termed *operational decisions* which are very well understood matters, often to the extent of being able to program a computer to recommend a particular decision. For example, stock control is a reasonably well understood process and given values for certain variables, such as the cost of keeping a particular item in stock for a certain length of time, a computer can perform a set of predefined steps and make the decision. It may be as a matter of choice that management decides not to do this and only allows the computer to recommend a decision, or even not to use the computer at all, but this does not change the fact that the decision is an operational decision. Information for such decisions is well understood, internally focused, predefinable and precise. Given that such decisions are made possibly many thousands of times per day within an organization, it would appear sensible to consider the use of a computer. John's task of authorizing salesmen's bonuses is an example of the use of this kind of information.

In addition to all of this information required for making decisions, a need exists to generate and manage the *operating data* of the business, for example accounting data, payroll data, order processing and invoicing data. These data are not required for decision making but must exist for the business to continue operating. Such data can be predefined, tend not to change very much through time and need to be very precise. The production of the invoices in the data processing department would be an example of such data. Notice how the data are not produced for management purposes – management would only become concerned if the data were not produced.

A third important classification of the systems is that all of the formal systems mentioned in John's day consisted of an input element, a process element and an output element – the process element may have some aspect of storage contained within it. The value to its user of any particular system will arise from one or a number of these elements. For example, the electronic mail system used by John, will have an input element, namely functions to assist with the composition of the message, a processing element which largely consists of a message storage and physical movement function, and an output function which allows the recipient to collect the message from any connected terminal and to reread all or some of the message as required. In these processes John was involved in the input and output processes. Compare this system with the invoicing

Some of the components would be seen traditionally as belonging to the discipline of data processing, namely the computers and the digital communication aspects, whereas others would not, for example the telephone and the telefax equipment. However, all of these aspects are part of information systems as defined in this book.

A fourth classification of information systems could consist of the source and degree of tailoring of the system. Some systems are produced especially for a single organization. John's competitor database was probably at least tailored for his organization to reflect the information it was wished to store. However, other systems, for example the electronic mail system, may be identical in John's organization to that used in many others, no tailoring of the system being necessary to satisfy the organizational needs.

The fifth and final classification of information systems to be discussed here focuses upon the way in which the system provides value to the organization. Additionally, it represents the evolution of data processing in many organizations, which is also illustrated in Figure 2.3.

Initial activity in most organizations concentrated on developing systems for the purpose of improving internal efficiency. Tasks that were already undertaken by clerks were computerized and in essence efficiency meant an intention to reduce staffing levels. Tasks such as invoicing, accounting and order processing were developed to mimic the manual activities replaced. The data processing department had been born (see stage 1 in Figure 2.3). Information technology tools were developed to meet the needs of such systems. As explained in Chapter 1, the problems were mostly technical and large numbers of technicians were recruited. Systems flexibility was not especially important as the systems developed did not change very much through time. In the case above the invoices produced in the data processing department would be an example of such information.

As time passed attention turned towards using the vast quantities of information stored in the computer for the purpose of management information. This type of information related to the internal workings of the organization, and thus the phrase 'management information systems' had been originated (stage 2 in Figure 2.3). Major problems developed because the tools available to develop systems were those first used for data processing. Flexibility was required by the users who wished to amend the system as their needs changed, however, the systems were inflexible and difficult to change. The answer to this problem was provided later by the personal computer and it became the fashion to supply a manager with a microcomputer and to support his or her technical needs but leave all development of the system to the manager. This tended to lead to fragmentation and duplication in systems as sharing data between departments slowed the development of the system and hence each department tended to develop systems independently yet using similar data. Additionally, some of the issues solved by the data processing professionals in the first stage tended to surface again, for example documentation of personally developed systems can be a little inadequate. However, even considering these problems many hundreds of systems were developed by some organizations. In the case above, the periodic international sales report would be an example of this type of information usage.

These first two stages endorsed the existing form of the business and did not make any significant changes to its form or structure. This two-stage pattern progressed into the early 1980s when a new era emerged with the discussion of using information systems for competitive advantage. In detail this could be achieved in a variety of ways and hence organizations tended to move directly from stage 2 towards stages 3, 4, 5, 6 or 7. The logical sequence of the move from stage 1 to stage 2 did not continue forward towards stage 3. In fact some organizations tried to move towards stages 3, 4, 5, 6 and 7 all at the same time.

Moving to stage 3 involved attempting to integrate by way of sharing data or systems between the various functions of the business. As an example, imagine a motor car manufacturer which decided to provide a very high degree of personalization on each car yet to maintain manufacturing costs within the mass produced sector of the market. The personalization would extend to choice of internal trim colour, a choice from six sets of wheels, four sun-roofs, etc. Altogether there would be some sixty 'options'. Truly the cars would be bespoke at little more than the cost of a mass produced car. Added to this a high level of customer service in every aspect would be vital as the cars were to appeal to the discerning customers. The information system to support this would allow a detail specification of the car to be produced in the showroom on a visual display unit connected to the manufacturer's computer. After specification the computer would try to locate such a car at other dealers, or attempt to locate one in the delivery system. If this was unsuccessful it would then schedule the car onto the assembly line if all the components were available, otherwise it would electronically chase missing components from the supplier and then schedule manufacture. When the system has decided how the car is to be sourced it will give the customer precise delivery data. All of the elements of that system are available to most car manufacturers, for instance most manufacturers would have an assembly line scheduling system, but the difference with this manufacturer is that the systems are integrated! Generally, organizations are beginning to realize that in some instances value is to be gained from integrating the information available to the business rather than fragmenting it into functional subsystems. Interestingly such systems can cause the business to change its form of organization: departments can amalgamate and responsibilities can be reallocated in line with information movement.

Turning to stage 4, the boundaries of the business are widening. Organizations have realized that to produce an order on paper, post it to the supplier who will then rekey it into the supplier's computer is slow and inefficient. Computers owned by different organizations are connecting to form networks to overcome these inefficiencies. Orders, invoices, product specifications and many other documents are being transferred electronically. This is very similar to stage 1 but now with an external (to the business) focus. The term electronic data interchange is used to describe such systems.

Just as stage 2 involved using information collected in stage 1, stage 5, electronic information interchange, involves organizations in sharing information. For example, rather than two organizations carrying stock of a particular item it may be advantageous for the stock level of each party to be available to all interested parties. Here it is not just moving the equivalent of electronic paper between suppliers and customers, but information is being shared between the parties to the mutual advantage of all.

Turning to stage 6, sharing information can lead to changing the form of who does what in an industry. Returning to stage 5, the sharing of information on stock levels may lead to just one of the organizations keeping all the stock on behalf of all parties and having the information available to all. As in stage 3, when it was said the form of the organization can be changed by information systems, so in stage 6 the form of the industry can be altered. Suppliers can take on tasks traditionally carried out by the organization.

As mentioned earlier executive information systems are being developed to provide the information required by top management. This may be both internal and external to the organization and may facilitate internal and/or external business integration. The issues associated with executive information systems are those of formalizing the informal. In most organizations today stages 1 and 2 would be found in place although redevelopment is a continuous process. Stages 3 to 7 may be under development but likely to be a relatively recent innovation. Having considered various classifications of information systems the next chapter will examine the issues involved in their development and usage.

3

Issues in information systems

This chapter highlights and explores some of the issues involved in managing information systems. It is included here because the constraints to the development of successful systems are seen by some as essentially technical and hence see the resolution as similarly focused. It is our view that some of the problems are technical yet a substantial number are organizational and managerial and that the proportion of managerial to technical problems is increasing and is likely to become dominant.

For many years the data processing department has been the scapegoat of organizational information problems. Sometimes the blame has been allocated correctly, however in some cases lack of direction from business management has caused problems to occur which manifest themselves in the data processing department. The identification of problems is vitally important to success. If the problems are of a technical nature then a better understanding of the technology is required. However if the problems are of a managerial nature, then the whole approach to resolving the problems will be substantially different.

This chapter first presents a situation, at length. Then the issues revealed are analyzed from the viewpoints of the individuals involved. Finally, questions are posed which form a basis for the rest of the book.

John Long and Son is an organization involved in the design, production and marketing of some 2,000 different games to 20,000 retail outlets. The company employs approximately 5,000 people at two major sites in the United Kingdom. The company has been using computers for twenty-five years and has a substantial collection of applications in use. A central development and operation unit is located at one of the central sites which supplies service to the organization. This unit employs forty staff. Microcomputers have been in use for the last five years and approximately 150 are in use throughout the company.

The data processing department spends some 65 per cent of its development budget on maintenance, and on analysis only a small part of this cost is true maintenance – the majority being spent on small systems enhancement and one-off reports. In an attempt to deal with the issues of one-off reports a project codenamed 'Camel' was originated with the intention of downloading data from the central computer onto microcomputers for subsequent analysis. For this to succeed a number of the basic applications on the central computer require substantial modification. Potential users were invited to the launch of this project but it was poorly attended to the point of embarrassment. Those who did attend were disappointed to hear that the project would take thirty months to complete due to overstretched development resources and the substantial redevelopment required of basic systems. It was generally agreed, however, that such a facility was required and that the project should proceed.

Peter Walker, a bright regional sales manager with a masters degree in business administration (MBA), had long thought that if he could reanalyze the sales information, benefits may arise by linking together customers who traded under separate names yet were part of a large group. Such information was on the central computer but not one of the sixty-eight sales reports available provided precisely the information required. He had heard on the grapevine that requests for new reports were being delayed substantially and sometimes such delays ran to twelve months! Peter had heard third hand that a new system due for delivery in three years had effectively stopped the development of new reports. However, business was a little quiet so Peter decided to try to develop this system himself. The first requirement was to obtain a microcomputer. This was not an easy task because all requisitions for such machines needed to be approved by the data processing department which always required detailed statements of requirements, costs, benefits and lots more information, most of which he did not have. Rather than tackle data processing, who no doubt would refuse his vague request, he consulted his brother, a civil servant who had an interest in computers. Taking the advice offered he went to the local computer store and purchased a laptop computer and a spreadsheet program. The official order specified a generalized piece of office equipment, but the computer store did not mind as long as they were paid! Peter put a great deal of effort into making the machine function but he put all this down to 'investment'. Slowly the analysis system came together, as a result of many hours of effort both at home and at work. However, Peter did not mind all this effort because he saw the task as a challenge. The rekeying of the sales data was tedious but for the moment he only did this for a very limited product range so that task was manageable. Some very interesting statistics were revealed by the analysis which he showed to his superior who was impressed but was only interested in the increased sales resulting but not in the system.

However, in the light of what they had learned it became obvious to both Peter and his manager that the system should be expanded to include all products and all customers. Peter knew his small computer was inadequate for such a task and so he interviewed three suppliers and chose a local branch of a national organization to supply a multiuser minicomputer with database software. It would have been very difficult to buy this machine, which was estimated to cost £25,000, without the agreement of data processing. He obtained the forms used when requiring a microcomputer and attempted to answer the questions, but even after his months of experimentation some were very difficult to answer. For instance, Peter was very unsure of the amount of management time that would be necessary to implement the system. However, he persevered even though this meant leaving many questions unanswered. In an attempt to involve the data processing department he requested assistance in completing the form, but the department was clearly offended that he had selected the hardware and software and was unhelpful. Two weeks after submitting the request a negative reply was received. Peter discussed this with his superior and it was resolved that Peter's superior would discuss the matter with the financial director, who was also responsible for the data processing department. The meeting was long and heated with the financial director asking for time for the new 'Camel' system to be completed. The sales department saw this as an unnecessary delay in receiving vital information. After much debate it was agreed that the sales department could proceed to implement the system as long as it did not affect any other system or other parts of the organization. However, this appeared to be an uneasy compromise.

Peter moved ahead very quickly purchasing the necessary equipment and software. The costs of the software escalated as the project progressed but this was seen as quite normal for an IT project because almost every other IT project the company had ever developed was delivered late and over the expected cost. However, within three months, the sales department had a six station multiuser database system operating, which was seen as a triumph, having received little help from the data processing department. In fact Peter was planning other applications that could use the spare capacity on the sales department's machine and trained one of the office managers in the development of very simple enhancements and even small new systems. The data processing department allowed this office manager to work in the department for two weeks to become familiar with the procedures necessary to operate the computer.

Six months passed with no major problems occurring. At a routine meeting between the financial director and Peter's superior reference was made to the new system and it was agreed that part of an accounting system developed some years before by data processing could be discontinued because it was duplicated by the new system. This discussion lasted barely five minutes.

A further six months had elapsed when Peter received a call from this office manager informing him that a necessary backup of a file had not taken place and it was impossible to process the statistics without a major reprocessing of all the year's sales data. It was estimated this would take up to a month of continuous effort. This presented significant problems to the accountants because they were now users of the data, the duplication of which had been stopped six months previously. The data processing department could not recreate the old system because the necessary data were not available and hence the accountants had a significant problem. When the matter was reported to the chief executive he professed ignorance of how computers work and claimed that nobody had even told him that the sales department had bought a computer. He was the chairman of the company's IT steering committee but had not attended any of its meetings for the past eighteen months. The reason he gave for this was that he did not understand the technical issues discussed at the meetings and hence considered his presence to be pointless.

Now to summarize the views of the participants – first those of the chief executive: data processing was not seen by him to be a major issue to the company and so he delegated the issue to the finance director whom he considered to be similarly uninformed. However, he knew the data processing manager was technically competent and paid him what he thought was a very large sum to look after such matters. The chief executive felt he could not be a specialist in all matters, but objectively, he was in neglect of his duties. What evidence was there that many more opportunities were available within the company for the profitable application of information technology? Could it even be that the company's competitors were planning to use the technology to create advantage? Had the chief executive created an environment in which such ideas could surface and be tested? Had the chief executive used the IT committee to control the activities of the specialists and to be sure that the contribution to the company was consistent with company direction? Had the chief executive co-ordinated the activities of functional groups or had he allowed them to pursue functional goals? Had he even created a sensible organization structure – for instance, did it make sense for the data processing department to report to an uninformed finance director? On all of these charges the chief executive was likely to be found guilty. You might think that no chief executive would ever control a company's IT activities in this way, but in the past such a separation of the IT activities from the business was not uncommon and the cynic would say that this attitude still prevails today.

Turning to the data processing department, its staff may well see the problem beginning with users wanting to take over their role – for instance, they might ask why Peter could not wait for the 'Camel' system which was under development. They had created rules that attempted to restrict the use of technology to tasks that could repay the investment, yet these rules were broken with little consideration for the effect. Nobody seemed to support them, not even their ultimate superior the financial director. They were only consulted after all the relevant decisions had been made, even though they were supposed to be the specialists. They even tried to help by allowing an office manager to observe the running of their computer. In summary, they may well hope that users have learned their lesson and will not attempt to do the jobs of others again. Such views could be expected in the circumstances, but what could the data processing staff be charged with? The rules of purchase appeared to be very restrictive – the prospective purchaser must know precisely what he or she wants and the exact benefits to be gained. It could be said that such rules would not encourage anything but the most straightforward of tasks which result only in labour savings. A second charge might be their unwillingness to be the minor element in a development team. Users 'doing it themselves' with just a little assistance from data processing staff is a growth area and quite a satisfactory method of development for some kinds of application. However, did the data processing department distinguish between application types? Nowhere was reference made to training being provided for users and it would be reasonable to expect this from a data processing department. Therefore, the data processing department was not blameless! Turning to Peter, he could argue that he nearly succeeded despite receiving little help from anyone. He developed and tested the prototype at great personal inconvenience. If he had followed the rules the innovation would never have got off the ground. Peter may consider that his only minor omission was not to train the operator who forgot to copy the lost data and even that was bad luck because the operator was a temporary employee standing in for the trained operator who was on maternity leave. To be a little more objective, a number of his comments make a great deal of sense and he was an IT innovator in a non-innovative organization. However, he should have been willing to share his idea with the data processing department earlier and in more detail.

Peter's manager would argue it was his job to provide facilities for his subordinates, and in this case it meant bullying the financial director into allowing Peter to continue to develop the idea. Therefore, in his own eyes he did a good job. Objectively, he might reasonably be expected to understand something about sharing data between his own and other departments and to insist that Peter co-operate with others in producing the larger system. He did not do this because he was not interested in IT, but then he never had been and he had managed to progress quite satisfactorily to date – old habits take a lot of breaking!

Turning now to the financial director, who could be seen as the chief culprit. He was probably an accountant by profession and possibly quite a good financial director and in his own eyes the data processing department was 'allocated' to him. He had allowed the development of the new system in an attempt to be flexible. If users want to be involved in systems development they must be allowed to do so – a comment he had no doubt heard at yet another 'hype' conference. He had stopped the production of the information in his own accounting department because it appeared inefficient to have two systems in operation producing similar data. Objectively, he had allowed a basic company system to cease operation when he had little information on the robustness of its replacement. Flexibility is one thing, stupidity is another!

The preceding paragraphs have outlined a situation in which every person involved appears to be trying to do their best but the outcome is catastrophic. What appears to be a technical matter, namely the failure to copy a file, is revealed upon examination to be more of a management problem. A number of questions have been posed which will be answered as the book progresses. Answers for an organization of the size and complexity of the one described can be dealt with intuitively, but this is not the case for large organizations. These need a framework within which these matters can be considered and this book will provide that framework.

The next chapter (Chapter 4) will discuss a framework that would, if applied, ensure that the opportunities underpinning the business strategy are pursued – the chief executive of our fictitious company should read this. Chapter 5 considers the tools which can be used to identify the opportunities available from IS – Peter, his manager and all the other managers within the organization would gain from reading this chapter. Chapter 6 proposes a framework which identifies how each type of application can be managed – the data processing staff, the chief executive and other senior managers would benefit from this chapter. Chapter 7 continues the theme of systems development and proposes a 'standard' process of development which can be tailored to suit individual needs. This would be of use to the data processing staff of our fictitious company, who appear to want to use the same development method irrespective of the type of application. Peter and similar managers would also benefit from this chapter. The following chapter (Chapter 8) brings together the issues from the previous four chapters (Chapters 4–7) and considers issues not otherwise covered elsewhere. Both data processing staff and the chief executive would benefit from this chapter. Finally, Chapter 9 considers IS and IT from the perspective of society and is associated only indirectly with the case explained.

4
Integrating information systems and business strategy

Introduction

In the past the IS strategy of many organizations was essentially the summation of existing activities and plans, often derived from the bottom-up development of systems rather than a coherent business driven plan. This piecemeal approach to IS probably resulted in missed opportunities and an inefficient use of resources. Success or failure resulted from the organization's ability or inability to deploy technology in providing good data processing or management information systems, without requiring any changes to the business or organization. However, this situation has now changed. Now the investments in IS/IT by outside parties – such as customers, suppliers and competitors – can require an organization to change its approach to managing IS/IT in order to avoid significant business risks and disadvantages. The lack of a coherent IS strategy can result in any number of the following problems:

1. Competitors, suppliers and customers may gain advantages over the organization.

2. Business goals will become unachievable due to systems limitations.

3. Systems are not integrated thus causing duplication of effort, inaccuracy, delays and poor management information.

4. Systems' implementations are late, over cost and fail to deliver

expected benefits due to lack of clear focus on key business needs.

5. Priorities and plans are being changed continually producing conflict among users and IS staff, and poor productivity.

6. Technologies chosen do not integrate and even become a constraint to the business.

7. No means exist to establish appropriate IS/IT resource levels, to evaluate investments and to set priorities consistently.

Therefore, in total greater expense than necessary is incurred to deliver less benefit than expected and IS/IT generates organizational conflict which wastes management time. These problems result in part from the inability of management to manage the demand for information or systems in accord with the business needs, and/or to manage the supply of systems and technology coherently, and/or to match the two successfully, as explained earlier in the book.

A strategy can be defined as *an integrated set of actions aimed at increasing the long-term well being and strength of the enterprise.* This chapter considers how the planning of IS/IT can become linked to the business planning process, and hence driven by the management, in relation to the business environment and goals of the organization. Based on frameworks derived from business strategic management, the ways of achieving the linkage are outlined. The need for effective organizational processes to establish an integrated IS and business strategy is also considered.

The context of IS/IT strategy

The business strategy of an organization is formulated by analyzing various external and internal inputs, by using a variety of techniques, to produce objectives, policies and action plans. Some of these processes will require the development or improvement of information systems. This statement of requirements (i.e., *what* needs to be done) then needs to be translated into technology-based solutions (i.e., *how* the needs could be satisfied). This basic linear relationship is at the core of Figure 4.1. Even this simple logic is not always reflected in the reality of the IS/IT planning of many organizations – the process is often driven from the bottom up by technologists. However, as Figure 4.1 shows, IS/IT can and should be considered in the process

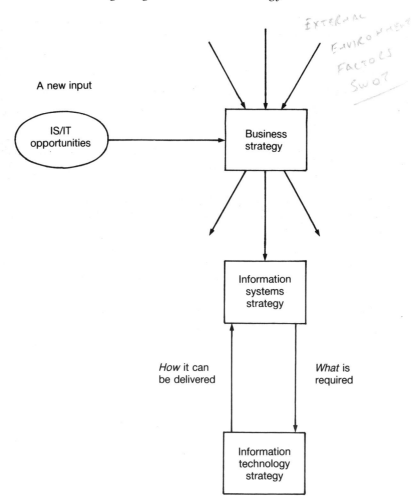

Figure 4.1 Information systems and technology strategy in context

of formulating strategy, in terms of what it can enable the business strategy to be. The potential impact of IS/IT on the enterprise in its business environment will depend not only on what it wishes to do, but also on what others are doing or are capable of doing. Integrating IS and business strategy must, therefore, include ways of assessing the potential impact which IS/IT can have on the organization and its business environment. This is just as important as considering other external environmental factors in formulating the business strategy.

Techniques for carrying out such an assessment are considered in the next chapter.

Based on this IS/IT input and other considerations of markets, services, products, resources etc. during business strategic analysis, areas for potential IS investment should be identified. Whether or not they are achieved will depend on how well those business requirements are converted to actual information systems and how well they are delivered through the IT strategy. Clearly the whole process is a continuous one, like any aspect of business strategic management, requiring monitoring and updating as results are or are not achieved and other business parameters change.

The chief components of IS/IT strategy can be therefore considered as the following:

1. *An information systems (IS) strategy* defining the information and systems needs for the business and its component functions. If the organization consists of more than one business, then each business will define such a strategy and in addition there will be a strategy for satisfying corporate requirements. The IS strategy should define what the business needs for the foreseeable future, based on an analysis of the business, its environment and the general business strategy. The objective is to establish the demand for IS/IT applications, aligned closely to the business plans and issues. These needs will change over time and the demand must be updated continually, reviewed and prioritized based on business imperatives. It may not be feasible to satisfy all these requirements, economically or technically, in the short term but over time more applications become feasible.

   This strategy must also define who, in organizational terms, is to be responsible for the achievement of the requirements, through the planning, development and implementation of the business systems projects and the relevant information resources.

2. *An information technology (IT) strategy* which defines how the needs will be met based on the priorities in the IS strategy. This involves determining how applications will be delivered and how technology and specialist resources will be used and managed in support of achieving the business needs. It will describe the activities which need to be performed, how they are to be organized and the means to be employed in developing and operating systems and in acquiring and controlling technology – i.e. how the supply can be achieved.

A corporate or general management responsibility is to balance the demand and supply issues to ensure that the business plans are achievable. This will require continuing reconciliation based on business priorities and supply constraints. In order to do this the organization must establish a process for integrating business and IS/IT planning.

IS/IT strategic planning – a process framework

While the strategic planning process is ongoing and iterative, during each stage of development or re-evaluation of the strategies it is important to have a consistent framework which is understood by everyone involved. The products of the process are business IS

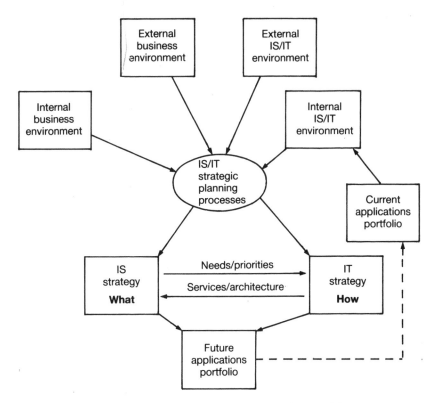

Figure 4.2 An IS/IT strategic planning model

strategies which define the needs and priorities, and IT strategies which describe the infrastructure and delivery services that come together to provide a future portfolio of IS/IT applications to satisfy the business requirements. To achieve the required outputs the planning process must incorporate all the necessary inputs. The old computer adage 'garbage in, garbage out' (GIGO) applies to the strategy as much as to an individual computer program. Given a comprehensive and relevant set of inputs, techniques of analysis can be applied together with some creative thinking to identify the best courses of action.

The four relevant inputs are discussed in more detail below, and are shown in the context of the overall process in Figure 4.2. Some of the tools and techniques of IS strategic planning will be discussed in more detail in Chapter 5. Before considering those detailed techniques this chapter considers how the overall process needs to be managed to ensure its long-term effectiveness.

The external business environment

This input is an assessment of the forces which are affecting the industry in which the business operates, the economics of the industry, its structure and competitive basis and within that the particular issues and pressures facing the business. This should normally be part of any business strategic analysis, rather than a part of a specific IS/IT strategic planning process. Based on such an assessment, the role that IS/IT is playing or could play in changing any aspect of the industry, can be examined to identify potential opportunities or threats. For example, the increasing power of retailers over manufacturing companies has been enhanced by retail point-of-sale systems and the information these provide for the retailer. Manufacturers need to consider how their IS/IT might be developed to either counter that pressure or perhaps better understand the potential of retail systems to gain some mutual benefit. Business environments are changing ever more rapidly, in some cases faster than the lead time for developing new systems. In such a case that speed of change needs to be reflected in reduced systems development lead times, which in turn will determine many aspects of the IT strategy – just as increasingly competitive environments impose constraints on product development lead times, and hence the methods of product design and manufacture.

The external IS/IT environment

This input consists essentially of two parts as detailed below:

1. The organization needs to appreciate and interpret the developments in information technology and the trends in both the economics of its use and the practicalities of applying new technologies to its business needs. An understanding of potential supply options and different vendors and their product offerings will enable more appropriate solutions to business needs to be considered and new application opportunities to be identified.

    Technology trends and developments needs to be evaluated both to select short-term options with a view to the long-term implications and also to plan when it looks most appropriate to intercept a new technology. When, for instance, would it be most appropriate to consider introducing electronic mail or image processing? No expressed need may exist but the cost of other forms of communication and document management must be compared over time with the ever improving economics of the new technologies.

    All new technologies imply some risk and a learning curve for the business. Early understanding, interpretation and selective use of developing technologies may enable a future advantage to be identified and obtained. How many organizations did not consider the long-term implications of personal computers? The result of this misunderstanding has often been excessive direct expense plus enormous, often hidden, organizational costs. If the need for more rapid development of new systems is not identified in time, the learning curve for adopting new systems development tools may be too long to improve the business situation. Often, the short-term expediency to continue using known technologies and tools continually overrides the long-term need to migrate to more appropriate technologies.

2. More specifically the organization needs to know how information technology is being employed by others within the industry, to what purpose and how successfully. In fact, knowledge of the use of IS/IT in other industries can provide a source of good ideas which can be transplanted. Most critically what the organization's competitors, customers and suppliers are doing must be interpreted in terms of the business implications. Using the example above, manufacturers of retail goods took a long time to appreciate

29

the business implications of the use of point-of-sales systems plus electronic data interchange and bar coding of products by retailers, and have had to react quickly to pressures from their customers and often at great cost.

A very successful flower auction suffered a short-term set-back when one of its competitors offered buyers the ability to buy flowers remotely through viewdata terminals. The competitor increased its potential market and in the short term attracted buyers away from the auction until the auction responded with a similar system. This illustrates not only the need to consider the available technology but also how it can be applied in the industry. In practice most companies which have gained strategic advantage from IS/IT have not used the 'latest' technology – it is too risky. They have innovated in a business sense, but used proven and well established, 'adequate' technology.

The internal business environment

This input consists of an analysis of what the business does, how it does it, and how it is organized and managed, in order to identify the information and systems needs. Such an analysis must be related to the external business environment and, again, this should be done as part of the business strategic planning process. In particular the following need to be considered:

1. The mission and objectives of the business must be expressed clearly together with the strategies being pursued in order to achieve those objectives. These will need to be interpreted accurately to define information and systems needs and also to set investment priorities. Often, an organization's stated objectives and strategies are rather vaguely expressed and not well understood by all the management. Unless these are more clearly defined the resulting IS/IT strategy will be equally vaguely focused and become subject to 'flavour of the month' changes which will continually disrupt the planning and implementation of key systems.

2. The business activities must be analyzed and the relationships and interdependencies understood. This analysis must be as independent as possible of the current organization structure. It should describe the main processes of the business which enable

it to provide customers with products and services, as well as what needs to be done to control and develop the business. This will lead to the definition of a business information architecture, which should be robust enough to accommodate any changes in how the business is conducted and organized. The same analysis may well reveal weaknesses in the current organizational allocation of activities which either better systems can address or which cannot be addressed without organizational change. Once this activity model is established it is important to describe the economic implications of the various activities in order to identify areas of high potential benefit.

3. The strengths and weaknesses of the business, and the reasons for these, need to be assessed and agreed. This process will include an analysis of the resources of the business – for example, financial, people, products, technology etc. – in order to identify where IS/IT can focus on exploiting the strengths and redressing weaknesses.

4. While the ideal information and systems model should be derived from a logical view of the business activities within the industry context, the eventual systems will have to be appropriate to the structure and style of the organization. Hence it is important to understand how the organization functions and how decisions are made in both the formal structure and the informal network of interpersonal relationships. This understanding will determine the type of information needed, who will need it and how it is presented and used.

Many structured management information systems fail to produce any benefits where the basic decision making processes are relatively informal and based on interpersonal trust rather than formal exchange of information. The rate of change of both organization structure and senior personnel will also determine the type of system and information required. While no system will ever be flexible enough to cope with all the complexity and variety of organizational relationships, the structure, culture and style of the management will determine how information systems are developed to support the management processes.

The internal IS/IT environment

This input consists of two main components, as follows:

1. The business systems and information resources which are in place and currently being developed must be assessed according to their contribution to the business. These need to be analyzed in terms of how effective they will be in the future and not based on historical needs. (Chapter 6 discusses in more detail how this assessment can be made by the business management.) The strengths and weaknesses in business terms of existing systems (the current applications portfolio in Figure 4.2) must be understood fully before further developments are undertaken, otherwise they may fail due to the inadequate foundations on which they may be built.

2. The IS/IT assets and resources need to be catalogued and examined in order to determine whether the current capability and technology of the organization are adequate for future needs. This is not just an audit of current technology (hardware, software etc.) but also a review of the people, their skills, how they are managed and the methods used to develop and support the systems and underlying technologies. One of the main reasons why IS/IT strategic planning studies often fail to deliver the changes required is that the organization is not capable of implementing the plans, due to lack of resources, skills or management process. One key aspect is understanding the culture and style of the IS/IT department and how it relates to the business culture. This reconciliation of the IS/IT approach and attitudes within the business environment is often a critical aspect of the strategy development.

In describing and analyzing each of these main inputs it is vital that agreement is reached among senior management so that everyone is looking at the same picture. Equally, issues that may arise should not be glossed over; they should be stated explicitly and become targets for resolution during the strategic planning process. If these issues are ignored at this stage, they will probably re-emerge and harm the implementation of the plans.

Processes for managing the strategy

Any strategic management process consists of three main stages and must incorporate two essentially different approaches. The three main stages are summarized in Figure 4.3.

Formal strategic planning

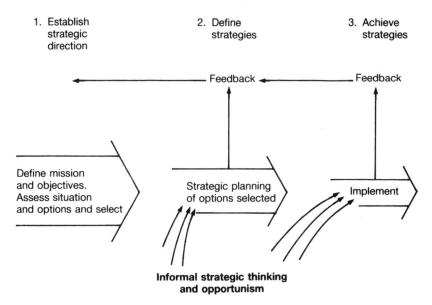

Figure 4.3   Strategic management processes

The two different approaches are formal and informal, which need to be balanced to enable creativity and ability lower down the organization to find the best way of achieving the objectives and strategic direction defined by the senior management. In Japanese industry in 1987 2 million employees made 48 million suggestions which were implemented and this is many orders of magnitude higher than in British companies. These suggestions are ways of improving what is done or how it is done within the strategic direction the management have set.

The first stage of the process is to establish the strategic direction by defining objectives and to select the basic means by which that direction is intended to be achieved. For example, a major manufacturing company defined its strategy as doubling its sales and profits in five years by means of organic growth in the United Kingdom, acquisitive growth in Europe, producing high quality products and providing the best customer service levels within the industry. This first stage needs to be understood and agreed formally at the highest levels within the company and also endorsed by major stakeholders, in the case of the example this was the parent holding company.

The second stage is to define specific strategies for the main areas of the business (e.g. marketing, distribution, manufacturing, R&D etc.) and turn these into viable plans by adding some more creative, informal thinking to identify the best way of achieving the strategy over time. Obviously there must be a feedback or control loop to ensure that the plans will take the company in the required direction, otherwise the various functions of the business may be heading in the wrong direction or worse still, different directions.

The third stage is to implement the plans in order to achieve the strategy. This will normally be done at some distance from the top management, preferably by everyone in the organization. Then the way the plans are to be implemented will be refined and improved by identifying new opportunities or better means of achievement. Again feedback and control are required, to ensure that 'local' adaptation is still enhancing the overall strategy, not deflecting it. To manage strategically the talents throughout the organization must be harnessed in the desired direction. Strategic planning produces little real benefit except perhaps to prevent wasted endeavours until strategies and plans are implemented.

All that has been said above in general terms about devising and implementing business strategies applies equally to the IS/IT components of those strategies. This means that mechanisms must be in place to establish formally the required direction, plan the developments and resource requirements and then implement the business systems and supporting technologies according to plan. Too often in the past the strategy was driven in reverse, for instance current projects were defined without reference to the business strategy, were built up into a plan and presented to management for ratification as a 'strategy'. Relatively informal thinking had dominated due to the lack of any formal senior management direction setting with respect to IS/IT.

However, the informal processes must not be stifled by a rigid planning process. Many of the most innovative uses of IS/IT which have resulted in competitive advantages have originated as opportunistic ideas from quite low down the organization. The feedback loop must also enable these ideas to flow back into the direction setting process since they may enable the direction set to be changed to advantage, thus some of the creativity in the informal thinking may make a significant contribution to the strategy. Therefore, whatever the means which are actually adopted to devise and then manage the IS/IT strategy, the senior management must initiate the process, set the direction and then demand feedback on progress and be receptive to new strategic opportunities. They also have a responsibility to signal any change in direction at the earliest moment to avoid major projects proceeding apace when the business reasons for which they were required are no longer valid.

While senior management must initiate the process it is also critical that line management incorporate the IS/IT plans into their more detailed functional plans. The new areas of strategic uses of IS/IT discussed in Chapter 2 require the business managers not only to identify and evaluate, but also to carry through the developments to success. The related business and even organizational changes must be planned and implemented successfully to gain maximum benefit. This all implies that line management and middle management must be involved actively and continuously in the planning and control of IS/IT implementation.

Establishing the IS/IT strategic planning process

While IS/IT strategic planning must become a continuing process integrated with business planning, two major problems remain for an organization wishing to achieve this long-term aim – given that this has not happened previously. The first problem is how to approach the development of the strategy in order to identify most precisely the business needs, i.e. what organizational grouping is the right level for the process to work? The second is how to carry out the process to develop the initial strategic plan. In both cases the following two issues are paramount:

1. The business and IT people who will implement the strategy must own it and hence must be involved actively in its development and understand its implications.

2. The process must be manageable, both in terms of scope and duration and deliver valuable results throughout the process, not just at the end. There must be clear checkpoints where agreement is reached and management endorsement obtained, before continuing more detailed analysis and formulation.

Both of these imply that whatever approach is adopted all parties, including senior management, line management and IS/IT professionals, must be educated before the start as to what is involved, how it is to be achieved and what the expected products are to be. A lack of

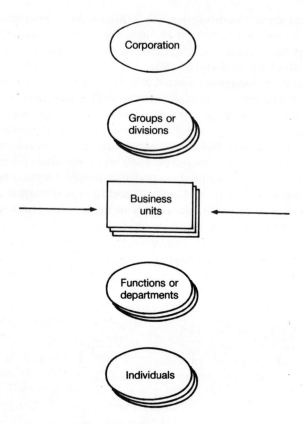

Figure 4.4 Appropriate level at which to develop IS strategies

mutual understanding and agreement on the objectives of the study at the start is a frequent cause of failure of such studies.

Addressing the first problem means that a coherent unit of the business has to be chosen for which an effective strategy can be developed. As with the development of business strategy, the appropriate level at which to develop a strategy is for a business unit (see Figure 4.4). A business unit can be defined as a component of the corporation that *sells a distinct set of products or services, serves a specific set of customers and competes with a defined set of competitors*. This may imply that organizational units need to be subdivided or even amalgamated in order to achieve a suitable strategic planning grouping, namely strategic business units. The starting point is taking an external view of what the organization does, not how it is structured to do it. This will enable the study to discover the particular business needs for information and systems within the business environment. Additional organizational needs can then be added to the basic requirements. Many companies are not organized into business units as described here. The component businesses may not be defined clearly within the organization structure due to historical or geographical reasons, or the use of the management talent available. It is important in the IS planning process to consider the logical strategic business units that the company comprises. Then the various techniques described later can be employed most beneficially. For example, a large house builder had three divisions – Southern, Northern and Scotland – but in each division it built two main types of home, namely low cost starter homes in large numbers and executive homes on small select sites. The information systems needs for each of these two strategic business units were different based on the design process, acquisition of sites, market place, cost structure and use of contractors etc. In addition each divisional manager needed systems to manage the region's activities profitably.

As has been said traditionally, the IS/IT strategy has been an amalgam of lower level functional, departmental or even individually determined plans for systems and technology which were driven mainly by internal, often localized, issues. Some organizations have attempted to develop corporate IS/IT strategies from the top down. However, the task is either too complex and hence takes too long, the business needs too various, or the environments are changing at different rates, which makes it difficult for a strategy that suits each component business to be developed. Equally importantly, the business unit managers do not own the imposed result. Even at a group level, unless the business units comprising the group are almost identical, considerable compromises are needed to achieve any common strategies. The net result is usually that only the lowest common denominator of needs is met by the strategy. This tends to omit the key areas of the business and focus investments on accounting, personnel and other less critical business areas. Figure 4.5 summarizes some of the implications of driving the strategy from a business unit or functional direction across the units.

The situation in Figure 4.5a, early in the process of developing systems, shows that due to economic arguments it seems sensible to use the invoicing system developed for business unit 1 in business unit 2, with some modifications, to deal with its particular needs. As more functions are computerized and a third business unit becomes involved the situation becomes much more complex. Having used

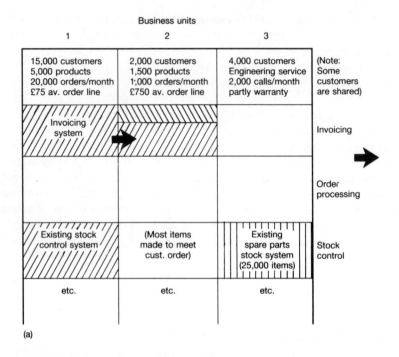

Figure 4.5 Demand (IS) vs. supply (IT) driven strategies in a multi-SBU company: (a) situation in year 1; (b) situation in year 3

the same invoicing system twice the economics are very attractive to use it again, in spite of further changes needed. In the meantime business unit 1 has developed an order processing system which links its invoicing and old stock control system. The third business unit needs a different type of link to its stock system and requires integration with its engineers call/despatch/reporting system, which means further amendments to the invoicing system. At the same time business unit 2 now wants order processing that links to invoicing (like business unit 1) but also direct to production planning. This implies large changes to the order processing system which business unit 1 does not need. In the meantime, business unit 1 has developed a new strategy to integrate all its systems by means of a product database which is unsuitable for either of the other business units.

Not only has a very complex situation evolved in terms of supporting the various systems, but also each unit cannot achieve its ideal systems without the agreement of the others. In the long term,

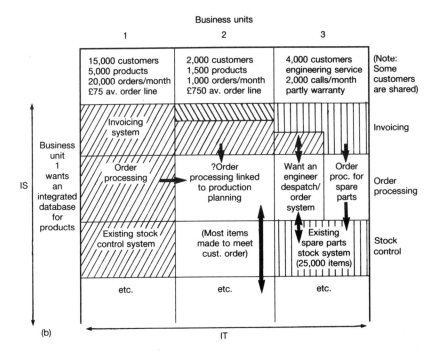

therefore, the costs increase dramatically and benefits may be reduced. In effect, the IT supply issues, especially short-term economies, have driven the strategy rather than IS demand side issues.

Within any large corporation different businesses may well be adopting fundamentally different strategies which will require quite different emphases in the information and systems required. Michael Porter identifies two principal ways in which a business can achieve long-term success. These are described as generic business strategies – 'low cost' and 'differentiation'. In a unit striving for lowest cost in its industry sector, IS/IT will be targeted at cost reduction primarily through simplification and automation. For differentiation, while cost control is still important, IS/IT investment will focus on enhancing that differentiation through such things as speed and quality of service. For instance, to achieve low cost a standardized order entry mechanism will minimize order handling costs. To achieve differentiation from competitors in the perception of the customer, it may be best to have a variety of ways of accepting orders, in ways which suit different types of customers. Equally, different policies for stock management, dealing with suppliers and management control etc. will be required to carry out the different generic strategies. (See References, p. 170.)

All of this leads to the obvious conclusion that different IS/IT strategies will be required for businesses in different industry environments, pursuing different objectives by means of different business strategies. If, in the example shown in Figure 4.5, the different business units were following different strategies – for example, one low cost, the other differentiation – then sharing systems would probably mean neither could pursue its strategy effectively. The overall IS/IT strategy for the corporation will be the composite of the strategies of the units plus the needs of the corporate and/or group business unit for information and systems. These will be based on the means by which they develop, direct and control the total business. There may also be synergistic opportunities across the business units which can be identified from a higher level viewpoint, especially where the businesses are similar and/or trade with one another. The IS strategy needs to be clearly focused on the particular, even unique, aspects of the business in its environment. When considering how the systems are to be supplied there may be further benefits in terms of economics and effectiveness of delivery by limiting the variety of IT strategies adopted, but this should involve the minimum number of business compromises from their ideal needs. Again if the strategy is predominantly driven by IT supply optimization issues, the business users will not own the strategy, nor will it meet their needs.

The means by which the first iteration of the IS/IT strategic planning process is carried out will undoubtedly influence the longer-term strategic management approach – for better or worse. In the worst case a planning study produces nothing of business value after a considerable time and at great expense. The majority of strategic studies may not be that wasteful and ineffective, but many do not deliver much of real value and do not establish a viable mechanism for the future. Some of the main reasons why such strategy studies fail are as follows:

1. Top management commitment to implementing the plan cannot be obtained.

2. The planning exercise takes too long for management to sustain

interest – it is also very expensive and takes up too much of the management's time.

3. The process produces an overwhelming amount of detail which is difficult to interpret.

4. The resulting plan fails to spell out resourcing and financial implications.

There seem to be three main approaches adopted for strategic IS/IT planning studies, namely:

1. Set up a special IS/IT planning function to carry out the task. This is normally located within the IT department, which then owns the strategy!

2. Employ consultants to bring in techniques and skills to facilitate the process. This is obviously helpful, but in many cases the consultants take over and produce the strategy in the form of a large detailed report, and again ownership is lost.

3. Set up a task force or steering group to carry out the task, preferably led by an experienced and respected business manager. While being the most difficult approach to establish, it is by far the best, since not only does the strategy belong to the organization, but also it is more likely to be truly business driven, be carried out efficiently, and likely to be implementable.

The third of these approaches is the one most likely to overcome the main reasons why such strategy studies fail.

Following the first iteration, a longer-term approach needs to be established. Ideally IS strategic planning should become an integral part of the business planning process. The IT strategy should be an appropriate set of responses to those business IS strategies. In addition an ongoing management steering mechanism will probably be required to reconcile the demand and supply issues which will arise continually.

Summary

At the start of this chapter it was argued that unless an organization has a strategy for its information and systems which is driven by the business requirements, a number of problems will ensue. These could result in the business being seriously disadvantaged within its business environment, and/or spending significant sums on IS/IT investments, but achieving few business benefits. That strategy must prioritize demand according to business needs and then ensure that the supply of resources and technology is managed in the best way to satisfy the demand.

To achieve a coherent IS/IT strategy the organization needs to establish a business driven IS/IT planning mechanism. The timeframe of the resulting strategic plan should reflect the business planning horizon – this can be five years or more in a stable business, but may be only one to two years in a volatile one. In most businesses achieving a two to three year IS/IT strategic plan would be the most feasible. However, the planning mechanism must ensure that it is a rolling plan which is updated regularly, even continuously, as achievements do or do not occur, the business situation evolves, and options change. This chapter has described in general terms the context and concepts of IS/IT strategic management. The next chapter describes a number of the tools and techniques which can be used by senior, line and IS management, working together, to identify what information and systems the business needs to gain the greatest benefits and maximum leverage from the opportunities which IS/IT offers.

5

Identifying business advantages from information systems

Introduction

The previous chapter described the business strategic context within which information and the systems required are to be identified and then managed successfully. No matter which process is chosen to establish the requirements, some tools or techniques will be required to analyze the business, its environment, strategy and activities, to select the areas where IS/IT offers benefits. However, the tools and techniques are only a means to an end and while useful they are not a substitute for creativity and experience. Hopefully they allow that creativity, even intuition, to be focused more effectively and the experience to be converted into successful future action. The objective is to determine business relevant applications of IS/IT which can improve business performance. This may involve improvements in efficiency of operations, in the quality of the management processes and even in the way the business is conducted or organized – and in some cases all of these.

This chapter considers some high level techniques which can be used to identify the *demands* for IS, based on the current business imperatives and longer-term potential opportunities. It is not an exhaustive or exclusive set of ideas, but is a set of tools and techniques which can be used by the management, users and IS specialists together to achieve an agreed view. Again no strict methodology for using the techniques can be defined which suits every set of business circumstances, but a planning framework will be described within which the ideas can be applied coherently.

The framework attempts to bring together three aspects of demand planning which need to be considered simultaneously to enable the resulting requirements to be reconciled and the most valuable selected for action. These three themes are as follows:

1. Situation appraisal to decide 'where we are now' in terms of the business and the information systems in place and their relevance in the future.

2. Creative opportunity 'spotting' to identify what the business could do with IS/IT – i.e. 'where we could be'.

3. Analytical assessment of what the business needs to do with IS/IT if it is to achieve its business plans and objectives – i.e. 'where we want to be'.

The result will be a portfolio of information systems requirements – a business-based review of the value of existing or past IS/IT investments, a set of known requirements to be satisfied in the near future, plus a set of potential IS/IT opportunities. The next chapter (Chapter 6) then considers how supply side strategies can be established to satisfy the variety of demands.

A planning framework for determining the requirements

The framework shown in Figure 5.1 describes the key steps involved in defining comprehensively the IS requirements for a business – i.e. the applications portfolio to be managed over time. The process is not as complex as it might first appear, but before considering the use of the various tools and techniques within it, the rationale for the framework structure needs to be explained. It illustrates the process – situation appraisal, analytical and creative – mentioned earlier. The framework is intended to be used to determine the requirements for a business unit as described in the previous chapter. By using the same framework for all units in a corporation, however, additional opportunities can be identified as will be shown as the techniques are explained.

The first stage in the process is essentially an extension of the situation appraisal required for developing a business strategy or

44

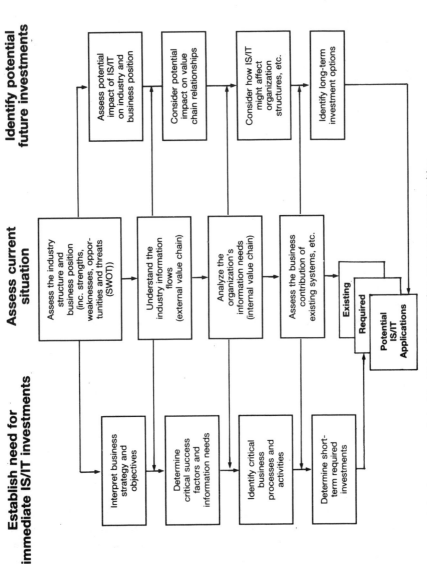

Figure 5.1 An approach to identifying information systems opportunities

plan. It poses questions as to whether improved information or systems could be used to affect directly the environment within which the business is operating and specifically the various competitive forces acting upon the business. This implies considering options available not only to the business but also to its competitors, customers and suppliers and how they might gain a relative advantage. It is essential to consider the strengths and weaknesses of the various parties in the industry in terms of their ability to take advantage of IS/IT. This leads to identifying potential opportunities and threats based on the potential impact which IS/IT could have on the industry and the balance of competitive forces. The situation can then be assessed in more detail using value chain analysis to identify the key information flows in the industry and how the balance of influence could be changed along the supplier-buyer links in the chain to gain an advantage. The external value chain understanding can lead to opportunities to link the business more effectively with the outside world by means of its information systems, the benefits of doing so and the consequences of not doing it. The internal value chain is a way of identifying the main information needs and flows associated with what the business does, rather than how it is organized to do it. Hence an ideal information and process model can be established as a basis for achieving the appropriate information and systems integration. This may lead to changed organizational relationships in order to exploit the new ways in which IS/IT can enable the business to operate or be managed. It is against this future model of the business requirements that the existing systems should be appraised, in terms of their functionality and how well they link the key related activities. What do the systems enable the business to do and what do they inhibit it from doing?

The product of this decomposition of the business relationships, activities and information-based processes will be a number of potential IS options for investment. However, this is not the whole picture, merely what could be done in time. What should be done in the next year or two depends on what the business wants to achieve in that period, and how it intends to achieve it. To do this the objectives and strategy of the business need to be interpreted to define short-term needs and select the priority areas from the ideas generated, namely those which could yield the earliest significant benefits.

This process is more analytical – a systematic review of the objectives to identify what is critical to achieving them and consequent information and systems dependencies. These critical success factors will lead to specific information needs and also identify the critical areas of business activity where improved systems will have the most benefit. Again it will expose weaknesses in the current information and systems which need to be overcome, if disadvantage is to be avoided. These will provide the criteria for selecting the key areas for immediate investment – i.e. the required plan of development, enhancement or correction. Other potential application ideas should not be rejected – some may well be worth further evaluation, even prototyping, and others may not be feasible in the short term but should be put 'on the back burner' for review in time or if certain business and technology factors change.

Each of the techniques is described in more detail below. This brief overview of the framework is intended to show how the techniques can be brought together to establish an overall picture of the potential IS options available to the business. The framework enables a number of important aspects of the contribution IS can make to be assessed by management, as follows:

1. The role IS/IT is playing and could play in changing the industry and relationships of the organizations involved can be considered before making internally-based decisions in isolation from the business pressures.

2. It enables creative ideas about the use of IS/IT, whenever they arise, to be evaluated against an information-based model of the business in order to decide on their relevance and importance.

3. It ensures that the IS/IT investment plan is driven by the business objectives and not local or even IT priorities.

4. It will enable partial reassessment later of any aspect of the requirements if any external or internal business or IS/IT factors change – which will happen inevitably.

5. It enables the existing IS/IT applications to be valued in a future rather than historical context.

Above all it is a business driven framework in which decisions about IS requirements can be arrived at and agreed by the business management. Its purpose is to establish a demand driven, opportunity seeking approach to the planning and control of IS/IT – which later can be considered in terms of how it can best be supplied. It is always important to decide what you want to do, before deciding how to do

47

it – although this has not always been the case in IS/IT planning. Each of the techniques is now described in more detail.

Assessing the business position within the industry in terms of IS opportunities and threats

In developing a business strategy the various products and services of the business are normally assessed in terms of their particular market situations and their strengths and weaknesses compared with those of competitors. Various techniques exist to make such an assessment. The simplest and most popular is the Boston Matrix, or business/product portfolio matrix, whereby products are considered in terms of their relative market share and the growth potential of the market (see Figure 5.2). This is based on the concept of a product life cycle of four stages – emerging, growth, maturity and decline – during which the relationship of demand to supply in the industry changes. The types of information and systems required will change during that life cycle and hence it is important to support each group of products in the different stages in the way that is appropriate to the stage of the life cycle. For instance, with new or emerging products demand is very uncertain, the market is ill defined, customer requirements need to be identified and matched with the product attributes and new channels of distribution may have to be developed.

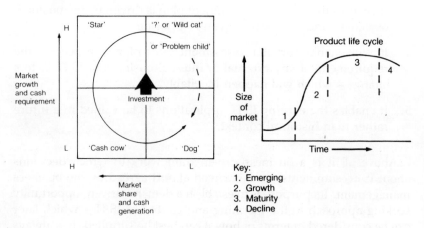

Figure 5.2 Business/product portfolio matrix

48

The information focus will be on market research and product development. At the other extreme, in a declining market supply will be greater than demand, the market and competition will be well understood and the objective normally will be to be very cost effective in serving the broad market, or to be selective and serve profitable niches. The information required will be very detailed in terms of demand forecasts, profitability of customers and products, and all aspects of direct and indirect costs will need to be controlled very carefully, not only to maintain profitability but also to release resources to invest elsewhere in the business. The types of system at the two extremes of the life cycle are quite different.

In growth and mature markets the information needs will change gradually as demand ceases to exceed supply and competitive pressures increase. In the Boston Matrix, successful products in growth markets are termed 'stars' and in mature markets are 'cash cows'. Star products normally will be an area of major investment to meet the growth in demand, for instance in marketing, capacity, developing distribution channels and in supplier relationships. Equally one would expect similar investment in information systems to help meet the required growth, especially to identify the demand and convert this into supply and resource requirements. Knowledge of costs and the profitability factors of the products, changing customer preferences and service expectations, and also competitor activity, will become important in anticipation of the growth reducing and the market becoming more directly competitive. At this stage the ability to satisfy a major share of demand is more critical than beating specific competitors. Systems must be able to support that growth and must not inhibit the ability to satisfy demand. It is also at this stage that good systems investments can create barriers to entry by tying in customers and suppliers and making entry to the market dependent on high up-front systems costs.

In mature markets, competitive rivalry will be intense and supply will gradually exceed demand. The objective is to at least retain market share and 'milk' the cash cow and reinvest the profits in new areas. This implies a more defensive investment strategy and IS can support this by enabling more accurate market segmentation, increasing productivity and optimizing working capital requirements (such as inventories) to match anticipated demand. Being more efficient and effective in using resources, suppliers and distribution channels, and building up customer switching costs, are all important, as is a detailed understanding of specific competitors' products, performance, strengths and weaknesses. Pricing policies will become more aggressive and critical and these need to be based on good market and cost information. In general, much more detailed control and planning is required. In many companies, while the business issues resulting from the product and industry life cycles are well understood, the translation into appropriate and then evolving information needs is less well appreciated. Many companies try to force-fit existing systems, often designed for mature products, to the high growth areas and they do not work well.

For example, a leading door manufacturer in the United Kingdom made two different types of doors, as follows:

1. Standard doors of some 200 designs sold through a catalogue to house builders, and by builders' merchants. The door manufacturer had a high market share and produced several million doors per year. This could be defined as a cash cow in a low growth mature market. The competitors were well known.

2. Speciality doors, such as safety, security and fire doors and high quality or odd size/shape doors. These doors were made to specification in small batches but were very profitable and had a reasonable market share, i.e. a 'star' group of products. The competition was much more diverse and included imports from Holland and Germany. The customers were also more dispersed and each purchased far smaller quantities, but the market was growing quickly.

The information systems had been developed to meet the needs of the volume business and were very effective in supporting a low cost strategy and the required automation, namely optimizing production, stock holding and delivery patterns. However, the systems did not really support the growing speciality door business where the objective was to differentiate the products on quality and service and hence justify a premium price. They had not been designed to support such a product range or customer base, but they were being used, ineffectively, to manage that part of the business. Consequently the available profit margins were not being achieved and customer orders were being lost. A more appropriate set of systems for this different and high growth area was needed.

In IS terms, the above door manufacturer should have been considered as two strategic business units with different business strategies and requiring different information systems. It can often be the case that from an IS perspective greater advantages can be

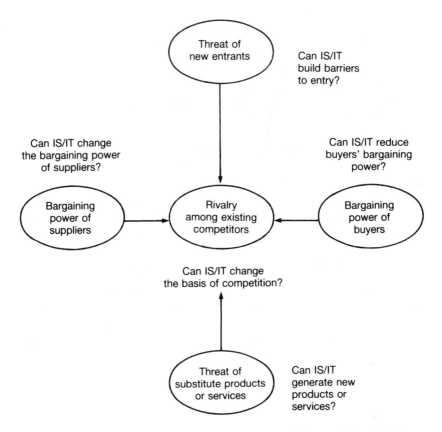

Figure 5.3 Analysis of competitive forces in an industry (after Porter)

achieved by considering the business in terms of different business units with specific needs than would be the case for other business or management reasons. Examples of reduced effectiveness by force-fitting systems from another part of the business at a different stage of development, or in a different market or competitive situation, or even pursuing an inherently different strategy, are all too common.

A further useful tool in such an analysis is provided by Michael Porter's approach to the appraisal of competitive forces in an industry to help define an appropriate overall business strategy. Figure 5.3 shows the key forces determining how an industry develops and which need to be assessed and interpreted if a business is to succeed in the long term. Added to the basic diagram are some questions to help in identifying how IS/IT might be used to assist in dealing with the various forces, to gain maximum advantage. The main objective is to ensure that IS investments are focused on aspects of the business which affect the competitive position directly. The first stage is to determine which of the forces pose a major threat to the future success of the business and in what way. Obviously IS investments are only one of many ways of then dealing with the issues that arise. Having ranked the various forces in terms of intensity of impact and immediacy of threat, the most critical should then be considered in terms of how IS could be used to gain advantage or avoid disadvantage. This tends to imply that the organization also understands what competitors, customers and suppliers are also doing with IS/IT or planning to do and what the effects might be. Often the action required will involve a relationship between two or more of the forces. For instance, establishing barriers to entry might involve increasing customer loyalty, increasing their switching costs and/or tying in suppliers more closely or reducing their bargaining power and hence making entry more difficult. The relationship between suppliers, the business and the customers will then be considered in more detail in the value chain analysis, details of which follow later in this chapter.

Threat of new entrants
The likely business effects posed by the threat of new entrants are that additional capacity will be introduced to the industry, the basis of competition may change and in the short term, at least, prices will be reduced. This can be counteracted in a number of ways by IS investments, such as by the following:

- Better control of distribution and supply channels to limit access.
- Segmenting the market to match the products of the business more accurately and providing a more complex target for the new entrants.
- Exploiting existing economies of scale more effectively to reduce costs in anticipation of a price war.
- Increasing the rate of new product innovation and development and/or differentiate existing products on quality or service.

In all these areas improved systems can help by providing better information, greater efficiency and an ability to react faster, by the use of computer-aided design (CAD) in product design, for example. As it has already been said, the actual cost of the investment in systems may increase the entry threshold, as has happened over the last ten years in grocery retailing, travel and financial services.

Threat of substitute products or services
The substitute may be a direct replacement (such as air for sea travel), or an indirect replacement in terms of customer preference (such as a holiday for a new hi-fi). In either case the threat of substitution will take the market into decline and produce more intense price competition, especially where fixed costs are high. Again IS can be used in a number of ways to counteract the threat including the following:

- Redefining market segments and products to match changing preferences and retain profitable areas.

- Improving the rate of product innovation to recapture preferences.

- Enhancing the products with new services to increase their perceived value.

- Improving the price/performance of the existing product by cost reduction.

- Identifying other new customer needs that can be satisfied, i.e. exploiting the existing customer base to develop new products.

Of course it would always be better to stay one step ahead by using the information available to identify changes in customer needs and be proactive on developing new products or services and increase the product portfolio.

Rivalry among existing competitors
Where rivalry among existing competitors is intense, generally in mature and declining markets, the effects are likely to be fierce price competition, increasing buyer power, more rapid product enhancement, and distribution and customer service levels becoming critical. These produce an obvious conflict in terms of cutting costs and increasing service levels. Without effective information systems costs can easily increase in such circumstances with service levels not improving – the wrong product is available at the wrong place and at the wrong price. Whatever IS is used for in this case, it must be deployed in support of the chosen business strategy – low cost, differentiation or niche marketing – in order to enhance that strategy effectively. A key aspect is to identify how IS can be used to reduce real costs, in relation to competitors, in all activities and relationships in the business – not by piecemeal cost custting. Another is to identify how IS can enhance the type of differentiation sought, whether that

be image, product quality, services provided – as perceived by the customer and end consumer. Getting close to not only the buyer but also the consumer of the product is important in order to understand their requirements and increase their loyalty and/or fear of buying less good products elsewhere.

Many retailers in highly competitive markets, such as clothing and DIY, have realized that product range, quality and convenience no longer provide sufficient differentiation to induce customer loyalty. Hence they have added further services, often using IS, to induce the customer to repeat buy (e.g. discount cards and financial services) and also to capture information about customers (e.g. where they live, who they are, what they buy and when).

Bargaining power of buyers and suppliers

How IS can be used to improve the position of the business in relation to the buyers and suppliers will be considered in more depth in the next section, but first it is worth summarizing the business effects when the power of each is high. When a supplier is in a strong position due to its size or the scarcity of what it provides, it can obviously increase prices, reduce the quality of what is supplied and make it less readily available, causing at best uncertainty and at worst an inability to satisfy customers profitably. 'For the want of a nail . . . the war was lost', as the story goes. Equally when buyer power is high, due to size, lack of differentiation in products available, or over supply, then prices will be forced down at the same time as a higher quality of product and service is being demanded by the customers and from the competing suppliers. One objective is to make it easier for the buyer – reduce the cost of buying, rather than the price of the product – to mutual benefit. The value chain analysis described below will explore these aspects more thoroughly.

The main purpose in this stage of the analysis is to focus attention on the business, in terms of its product portfolio and in relation to key external forces, to identify the different ways in which IS could affect the relationships and competitiveness, not only of the firm but also others within the industry. This can be used both to generate ideas and to identify whether current investments are related to the business opportunity areas or are major threats to success.

Value chain analysis

Value chain analysis is one of a number of techniques which enable management to analyze the role information plays in the industry, in the relationships between organizations and in the business itself. This can show the organization what information it needs to obtain, where that might come from and also how better or extended systems within the organization or in conjunction with suppliers or customers might improve its competitive position. Value chain analysis is again a tool to help define business strategies in terms of how best or how well the organization can add value and how it incurs cost – namely, the extent to which it can sustain its position in relation to customers, suppliers and competitors within the industry structure.

For every industry there is a value chain – a set of relationships between organizations which each take in resources of various types to produce something of greater value which is required by someone else at the next stage in the chain. Obviously in doing so, the value added must be greater than the cost incurred or a loss is suffered. In every case a matching of supply and demand must occur at the various stages of the chain in order to provide the required product or service at an appropriate cost. Within any industry there is a finite demand in terms of how much of the product is required and how much will be paid for it, and also at any time there is a finite supply of materials and resources to produce the product or service. Organizations compete not only with companies doing much the same thing but also with others along the chain for a share of the revenue, and hence profit, available within the industry. That amount of profit can be increased overall if throughout the chain demand and supply can be matched more accurately. Any business which operates at some distance from the eventual demand and also from the supply of key resources has to deal with considerable uncertainties and will find it difficult to optimize its performance. If, relative to its competitors, it can capture better key supply and demand information, it can optimize its performance relative to the competitors' uncertainties.

In non-profit making organizations or public bodies the income may not be generated by the services provided. Income is probably indirect, through donations or taxation. However, there is still a value chain and the organization's costs must be kept to within the funds available. It may not compete for customers, but it does compete for available resources, which could be used elsewhere. Recently many United Kingdom public sector activities have been forced into competitive environments by government policy.

This view of information at an industry level will highlight the key flows of information which the business needs to intercept and influence, from which its information needs can then be assessed and defined in more detail to determine the requirements for information systems. Many industry value chains are very complex involving manufacturers, distributors, service providers, sources of skilled staff and capital as well as raw materials, equipment and buildings etc. It is not intended that a detailed model of all these is produced, but the key dependencies and associated information which affect the success or failure of the business within the industry structure should be the focus of attention.

The external value chain

Figure 5.4 depicts a schematic, simplified value chain for a manufacturing type industry, which can serve to exemplify aspects which will apply to many organizations. There is a continuous exchange of information going on throughout the chain of which the business is only a part and therefore has only a limited view. A large corporation may own businesses in more than one part of the chain – clearly such an organization has major opportunities, by sharing information or by developing effective intercompany trading systems, to gain advantages over more focused rivals. However, in many corporations which are managed on profit centre lines, the links between component firms are often considered to be external. In any case, there are significant mutual advantages to be gained by firms linking their information and systems along the chain whoever owns the other companies.

A number of long-term benefits arise as follows:

1. Given that at any time the industry can generate a certain amount of net profit, that profit is shared among the various organizations in the chain.

2. If, in the version of the chain which includes our business, the overall net profit can be increased, we can take an increased share of that profit and hence outperform our direct competitors.

3. Information systems can make that happen particularly where demand and supply can be matched more accurately.

4. To do this normally requires the co-operation of suppliers or customers to provide that information and hence they would expect some benefit in return.

5. If the benefit generated is shared by us with our key customers

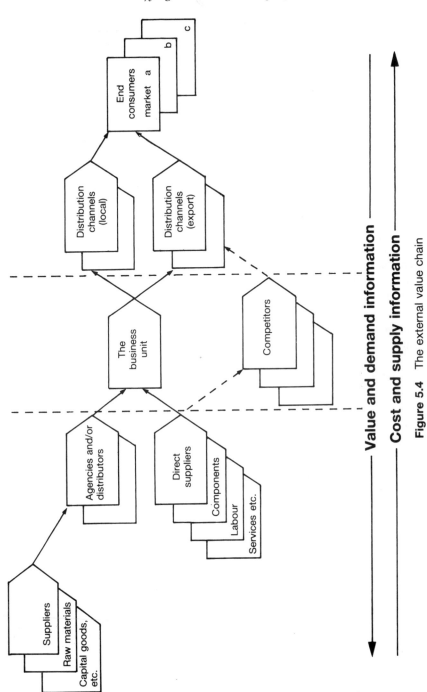

Value and demand information

Cost and supply information

Figure 5.4 The external value chain

and/or suppliers, then everyone can become more profitable provided they are part of 'our' more efficient or effective version of the industry. For such systems investments to succeed, the benefits need to be shared in order to gain long-term from buy-in to the system.

6. Assuming that rival firms are competing for the same resources and supplies and/or customers, their position will be weaker. Suppliers will prefer to sell to our business – because they are more profitable when they do – hence prices to competitors will increase or service levels reduce to achieve the new level of profit available elsewhere. Equally, customers will prefer to buy from us – it is more beneficial – and will expect either low priced products or better service from competitors.

The net result can be competitors facing increased costs and lower prices, and poorer supply service while higher delivery service levels are demanded, leading to a long-term, sustainable advantage for our business. That sounds easier than it actually is to achieve and in most cases only part of the advantage may be realizable with some suppliers and some customers.

How can information systems produce such mutual benefits? Consider any one interface between two organizations in the chain. The basic relationship is that of buyer and seller, placing orders, taking delivery, testing and eventually paying for the items. This involves considerable administrative cost and processing of data by both parties. These costs can be reduced by doing things only once, often by using electronic data interchange (EDI) between computer systems avoiding clerical effort, delay and potential inaccuracy. No doubt both parties hold stocks of the same items in order to satisfy demand or in case of supply problems. That duplication of cost can be eliminated by giving each other access to stocks available and by planning requirements ahead of orders. This could even result in links between scheduling systems to optimize capacity use between the two organizations. Joint quality control systems can be used to avoid duplicate or inconsistent checking resulting in unnecessary cost or waste. New product designs can be worked on in parallel using shared CAD systems to speed up the development of new products. Payment systems can be optimized to ensure both parties avoid the need for expensive short-term finance. Therefore, overall costs can be taken out of the interface and each firm is able to perform more effectively, hence generating mutual benefits.

Many organizations have been doing some of these, sometimes in active co-operation, but sometimes because the more powerful one wants it to happen. DIY retailers have moved on from basic EDI transaction exchange to joint stock planning and optimized delivery logistics. Suppliers who cannot or will not co-operate have to find other outlets for their products. A major oil company operates a joint stock management system with its main steel supplier at its North Sea depots. The stock belongs to the steel supplier but is used as and when required by the oil company and paid for as used – forecasts of demand enable the steel company to maintain appropriate stock levels at the depots. Many retailers who have installed point-of-sale (POS) systems can obviously exert leverage back through the chain by the knowledge of exactly what is bought and when, enabling them to hold the ideal range and quantities, and demand just-in-time (JIT) replenishment by suppliers. For further advantage, however, retailers need to know what is not bought and why, for instance, lack of availability or too high a price. Identifying this further part of demand is more difficult, but it is a help to both the retailer and the suppliers if it is shared. The main danger when the co-operation is one sided and the benefits are taken by one party is that the supplier cannot survive. In the long term, reducing the number of potential suppliers will change the balance of power once more.

The situation is not always best resolved in such a direct systems relationship. A kitchen manufacturer built excellent internal systems which enabled it to outperform its rivals in terms of speed and accuracy of delivery to consumers' orders. The consumer dealt with a retail outlet which ordered the kitchen from a distributor, which in turn bought from the manufacturer. Initially the advantages did not materialize – the distributor was more interested in selling the stock held than encouraging the retailer to sell the products it could most easily order and hence held less stock of. Only when the retailer could share in the benefits of placing orders direct to the factory did sales increase. The distributor became merely that – someone who was paid to move the finished goods to the retailer or customer for fitting.

A timber importer identified a key factor which affected timber prices outside his immediate industry sector. The number of housing starts in the United States (mainly timber framed houses) determined how much Canadian timber was bought in the United States and hence in a three to six month timeframe how much timber would be available for export to Europe. A model was built which monitored the number of housing starts in the United States and could forecast likely timber prices several months ahead, giving the buyers a distinct advantage when negotiating with other sources.

As a final example, a lighting company provides lighting specialists with a computer system to help design lighting systems in new buildings. The designers do not buy the lighting systems but influence the contractors, who buy from wholesalers, who in turn buy from the manufacturer. By providing the computer system the manufacturer can ensure that its latest products are favoured by the designers who can easily convert the design into a specification and components list for the contractor. In turn the contractor can most easily satisfy the contract by buying the components from one wholesaler who the manufacturer ensures holds stocks of the latest products in appropriate configurations to meet the designs.

This brief overview of external value chain analysis from an information perspective is intended to show how by examination of key flows of information in the industry, opportunities for advantage can be identified. As EDI becomes more easily and more extensively available it offers major advantages to those who can understand the changes in relationships it can bring about. Its use implies co-operation with others in the industry, even with competitors to agree standards, if the benefits are to be obtained. Equally importantly, before considering the information and systems required within the organization, the systems of gathering external data and exchanging information with trading partners must be established, or the internal systems will not fit the external environment.

The internal value chain

This is a way of considering how the various activities and functions in a business unit contribute in terms of satisfying the customer's requirements, and also how costs are incurred. What is done, how and how the activities are related will lead to information and systems needs and opportunities. It is a way of analyzing the activities in relation to the business, not in terms of how they are currently organized. The original model value chain described by Porter (1984) was based on a manufacturing business model, but the key groupings of activities can easily be translated to most other types of business. The model distinguishes clearly between two different types of business activity – primary and support activities.

Primary activities
Any business unit carries out primary activities to fulfil its value

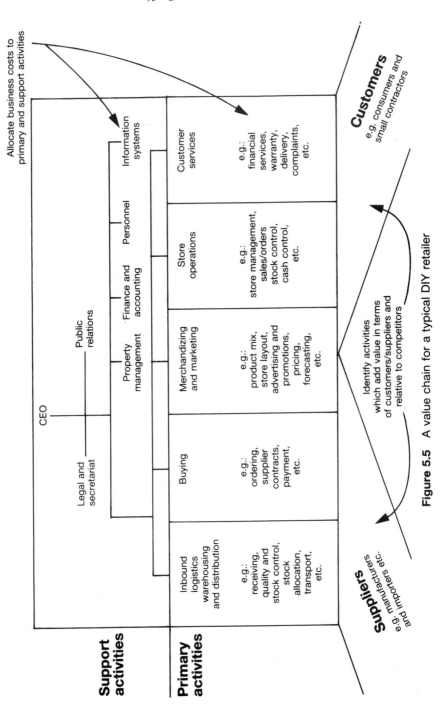

Figure 5.5 A value chain for a typical DIY retailer

adding role in the industry as required by its suppliers and customers. These primary activities must each be carried out successfully but must also be linked together effectively if optimum overall performance is to be achieved. This involves considerable exchange of information through the chain. The classic groupings of these activities can be considered in a sequence starting from dealing with suppliers and ending with the customers, as follows:

1. **Inbound logistics**: obtaining, receiving, storing and provisioning key inputs and resources to the main operations of the business. This can include recruiting staff as well as buying materials and services, dealing with subcontractors or equipment maintainers.

2. **Operations**: transforming inputs of all types into the products or services to meet customer requirements. This involves bringing together the requisite materials, resources and assets to produce the right quantity and quality of products or services – for instance in a university, delivering the courses in the prospectus and examining the students.

3. **Outbound logistics**: distributing the products or services to the customers either directly or through distribution channels, or the means by which the customer can obtain the product or service and pay for it.

4. **Sales and marketing**: providing ways in which the customers and consumers are made aware of the product or service and how they can obtain it, i.e. induce them to do so by promoting the products in a way that persuades the customer that it satisfies a need at an appropriate price.

5. **Services**: which add additional value for the customer at the time of or after the sale, such as financial services, warranty, training in its use etc.

A value chain for a typical DIY retailing organization is shown in Figure 5.5. The groupings differ from those above but the rationale of the structure is consistent in terms of the supplier-to-customer linkage.

In other service industries the main operation is less obvious – in a building society for instance there are a number of businesses, the main two being customer savings and mortgage lending. They relate to each other in terms of the use of the available funds. The main operation of both businesses is funds management ensuring that both lending and borrowing customers benefit from the society. These two value chains are inextricably linked and neither can be considered separately.

Support activities

Support activities are those required to control and develop the business over time, thereby adding value indirectly – a value which is only realized through primary activities in terms of business results. In a multibusiness unit organization some of the support activities may be shared by a number of businesses for economic and effectiveness reasons, the degree of sharing depending on the business similarities. In most cases some will be shared and others provided within the unit.

In many ways a business does not always have much choice over what its primary activities are, since they are heavily influenced by the nature of the products, customers and suppliers in its industry – what is critical is how well it carries out each activity and links the activities together, in terms of the profit made from the value added less costs incurred. Often information intensive activities such as forecasting, capacity planning, scheduling, pricing and costing must be linked accurately throughout the chain if each activity is to be carried out effectively.

A business does, however, have control over how it carries out its support activities and, from a corporate viewpoint, whether they are shared central services used by the businesses or delegated activities within each of the units. It is a matter of choice, which has to balance the need for managerial consistency across the units and the particular business situation and unique aspects of each unit. Either way the support activities have two main contributions to make – whether it is accounting, personnel, information systems, property management, legal, R&D etc. – as follows:

1. To enable the primary activities to be carried out at optimum performance levels, i.e. as a service or to develop new products or technologies or resources to meet business needs.
2. To enable the business to be controlled and developed successfully over time, i.e. as a support for the management through improved methods or better anticipation of the future.

Often, however, the support activities can actually disrupt the smooth running of the business by spreading their tentacles of control throughout the primary activities – this is the 'sales prevention system' often referred to by marketing people, or just 'the system'.

It is important to understand where all the costs of the business are actually incurred and why and how they are managed. The value chain model offers a useful way of allocating all the real costs in order to identify where savings can be made or where performance needs to be improved. Often continuing investment in one area, say manufacturing productivity, is pointless unless other activities are improved, such as sales forecasting. All the costs belong somewhere and every activity should be adding value, either directly or indirectly. If it is not, then it should be eliminated not computerized.

From an information systems perspective the internal value chain is a valuable way of identifying where better information and systems are needed, especially to show where integration through systems could provide potential advantage over competitors (or reduce current disadvantages). This may result eventually in changing the organizational structure to reflect the better way of operating and managing related activities. The logical approach to identifying how IS can help the business is by assessing the options in the following order by:

1. Improving relationships with customers and suppliers in all aspects of their interface with the organization, (e.g. integrated customer information).

2. Improving the critical information flows through the primary activities, namely removing bottlenecks and delays, ensuring the accuracy and consistency of information used (e.g. total stock management, customer service monitoring).

3. Improving the systems within each primary activity to achieve local improvements in efficiency etc., e.g. warehouse control, fleet management.

4. Improving the way support activity-based systems can best assist the primary activity management as well as meet central requirements, e.g. budgetary control, personnel data.

5. Improving the efficiency within the support activities by local systems development, e.g. financial consolidation, asset registers.

This may sound perfectly logical – driven from the outside, dealing with the critical parts of the business before the non-critical etc. – but it is almost the reverse of the approach to systems investments in most organizations taken over the last thirty years. The result has been that armies of people (often 10–20 per cent of all the 'white collar' people employed in many organizations) sit on the boundaries between activities and systems, reconciling information all day long! There is scope in most organizations not only to save money but also to improve the value adding capability by using more appropriate information flows.

Using the value chain analysis approach will force management to ask searching questions about the strengths and weaknesses of existing systems as well as identify key areas for future investment – especially to integrate the activities of the organization more successfully. The method of analysis, like many similar techniques has several key aspects, as follows:

1. It follows through the business unit approach to assessing business requirements and therefore links to its strategy.

2. It is independent of the current organization structure and clearly separates primary and support activities in terms of criticality of systems needs.

3. It concentrates on why the business is there – to add value to satisfy the customer and this enables basic questions to be asked about the activities and systems, such as how can it be done better, or cheaper, or both?

By considering the way information flows and is used in the business, in the context of the industry external value chain, the organization can identify the potential aspects of the business and its relationships that can be improved by better information systems. Some such process of analysis is also essential if the two remaining techniques described below are to be used to maximum benefit.

Information analysis

Value chain analysis produces a high level picture of the key external and internal business information relationships and issues. Before these areas of need can be addressed actively, a more detailed analysis or modelling of how information is collected and used by the various activities within the organization is needed. This will identify where data originates from (inside and outside the business) and hence who should be responsible for its management, who uses the

Key information entities examples \ Main business activities examples	Pay suppliers	Order materials	Receiving and QC	Stock control	WIP management	Production control	Order management	Finished goods control	Delivery/invoicing	Credit control	Retailer selling	Pricing	Sales forecasts
Outgoing cash	✓	✓	✓										
Supplier invoice	✓		✓										
Purchase order		✓	✓	✓									
Stock (RM)		✓	✓	✓	✓								
Production plans		✓	✓	✓	✓	✓							✓
Direct labour					✓						✓		
Product costs					✓	✓		✓				✓	
Product BOM		✓		✓	✓	✓	✓	✓				✓	
Replenishment orders					✓	✓	✓	✓					
Warehouse stock						✓	✓	✓	✓		✓		✓
Customer order							✓	✓	✓	✓	✓	✓	
Discount								✓	✓	✓	✓		
Invoice/del. note								✓	✓	✓	✓		
Customer							✓		✓	✓	✓		
Salesperson											✓		✓
6 month forecast								✓			✓		✓
Incoming cash									✓	✓		✓	✓
Consumer insurance													
Product repair etc.													
Indirect costs	✓			✓	✓	✓		✓		✓			
Gross profit	✓				✓	✓		✓		✓			
New product plans											✓	✓	✓
Financial returns	✓							✓	✓	✓			
Indirect labour			✓		✓	✓							

Primary activities in value chain sequence

Figure 5.6 Information analysis – relating business activities to information entities

Identifying business advantages from IS

Key information entities examples / Main business activities examples	Market analysis	Competitor analysis	Service order proc.	Spare parts mgmt.	Equipment services	Customer complaints	etc.	Expense reporting	Personnel/payroll	Management accounting	R&D	etc.
Outgoing cash				✓								
Supplier invoice				✓				✓	✓			
Purchase order				✓			·	✓				
Stock (RM)										✓		
Production plans				✓								
Direct labour					✓			✓	✓	✓		
Product costs				✓						✓		
Product BOM				✓	✓							
Replenishment orders				✓								
Warehouse stock				✓						✓		
Customer order	✓		✓									
Discount	✓	✓						✓		✓		
Invoice/del. note	✓		✓									
Customer	✓		✓		✓	✓						
Salesperson	✓	✓						✓	✓			
6 month forecast	✓	✓								✓		
Incoming cash				✓						✓		
Consumer insurance			✓	✓	✓	✓						
Product repair etc.			✓	✓	✓	✓						
Indirect costs								✓	✓	✓	✓	
Gross profit										✓		
New product plans	✓	✓									✓	
Financial returns										✓		
Indirect labour					✓			✓	✓	✓		

Support activities

67

same data and for what purposes, which in turn helps to define the need for databases and access to them; which process must be carried out first or whether processes can be carried on in parallel, to determine system interdependencies and timing requirements; and finally, it helps to determine whether organizational responsibilities are suited to the information view of the business, for instance, perhaps activities and responsibilities need to be reallocated or the organization changed.

From this more detailed analysis, a logical plan of development can be determined. Each project can be tackled in the most appropriate way (as will be considered later in this book), but within the context of an overall information model of the business, which shows how the systems will interrelate.

It is important during this stage of defining the requirements to follow through the rationale of the value chain analysis. The external data required and information relationships with suppliers and customers should be addressed first, followed by the linkages through the primary value chain and its contained activities. Once this stage is thoroughly understood and no key items have been omitted and duplication of tasks or data have been rationalized, then the requirements of each of the main activities can be analyzed within the overall context. It then follows that the support activities should be assessed in terms of the control functions and also the way they can enhance the performance of the primary operations.

The techniques for carrying out such an analysis of the business are essentially high level versions of the techniques of structured systems analysis, namely to define for a system the key processes, data requirements and relationships. They can be used at a higher level, with less precision, by teams of mixed skills, such as business people and systems professionals. The high level models – key data items, activity and data flow diagrams and matrices showing the interdependencies – are then key input to the more detailed stages of analysis and design on each resulting system development. An extract of one such matrix is depicted in Figure 5.6, which shows in summary which main activities use which key items of data. This would probably show more details such as where the data are created, where they are amended and where they are used. It shows that although it is possible to consider activities in the value chain sequence there are always considerable information overlaps as well as exchanges and feedback loops between activities in the major subdivisions of the chain.

Such a matrix along with a number of other models, including some showing how well existing systems and databases meet the future requirements, enable the following:

- A data model to be developed which satisfies the need to share, exchange and use data in the most effective way. Integration of data for all purposes is very difficult to achieve – this type of modelling will define where it is essential, desirable or not really necessary. Importantly, who, or what function in the organization, is to be responsible for the integrity of those data can be identified.

- The data flow diagrams will reveal the way processes relate to one another, can possibly be rationalized or reorganized, and also where major costs or delays are occurring – i.e. areas of potential benefits. Without such models it is not easy to identify offset benefits, i.e. those which will occur somewhere else in the organization due to a systems change in one department. For instance, earlier collation of sales data may give buyers more time to negotiate better supply contracts. The buyers may not be interested in the detailed analysis of sales, merely the major components they have to provision. Selected early, even crude data may be more useful than comprehensive, well presented, but delayed precise information.

One unexpected benefit of such an analysis is to identify unrealized potential in existing systems and data in the context of the future business needs. Weaknesses are to be expected but strengths are often revealed. In one organization a system deemed to be virtually useless was realized to have new potential uses. The problem was that over time the knowledge of what the system did had decayed, and only one person was still using all of its features. By this person retraining the others and developing better user documentation a major redevelopment was avoided and benefits were achieved very quickly.

It is beyond the objectives of this book to describe the various tools and techniques of information analysis in depth, and much has been written about them elsewhere. However, it is worth stating that such an analysis will produce enormous amounts of information itself – lists, definitions, flow diagrams, matrices etc. It is important that this is not done too soon, i.e. before the level of understanding of the business information relationships is established, otherwise the key requirements will be lost in a mass of detail. Equally it is important not to get lost in a mass of paper as the analysis proceeds. Therefore, some technology support is essential and there are now many software packages, admittedly of variable quality and comprehensiveness, available to help in this task. The models will have a long life but need to be amended gradually over that life. Poor documentation of systems has led to enormous unnecessary cost over the last thirty years. Poor structuring and poor documentation of the business's information resource could not only produce high costs but also lead to lost opportunities in the future.

Critical success factor analysis

The various approaches described so far have shown how the business can be analyzed to identify how new or better information and systems could improve its performance in the expected business environment. However, little account has been taken of what the management want the business to achieve in the short, medium and long term – i.e. the objectives which have been set. By analyzing these specific targets new information and systems needs may arise, but also the short-term objectives should be the means of setting priorities from all the systems investments which could be made.

Before describing how this can be done, the terms involved need some definition (the key relationships are shown in Figure 5.7). These are as follows:

- **Mission statement**: a broad statement that provides a general framework within which the corporation operates, which normally expresses the beliefs of the management as well as the long-term aims of the enterprise. For example, 'the company is a leading retailer of petroleum products and aims to ensure an equitable distribution of the results of increasing productivity among its shareholders, employees and customers'.

- **Objectives**: are specific targets for the business (or function of the business) which are expected to be achieved in a particular time scale – where possible they should be quantified and must be measurable in some way. They are what the business wants to achieve in a given time scale, normally one to two years, although longer-term objectives can be set. Following through the oil company example some objectives might be:
  (a) to achieve 2 per cent improvement in market share;
  (b) to extend outlet coverage in Scotland and Wales to levels elsewhere;

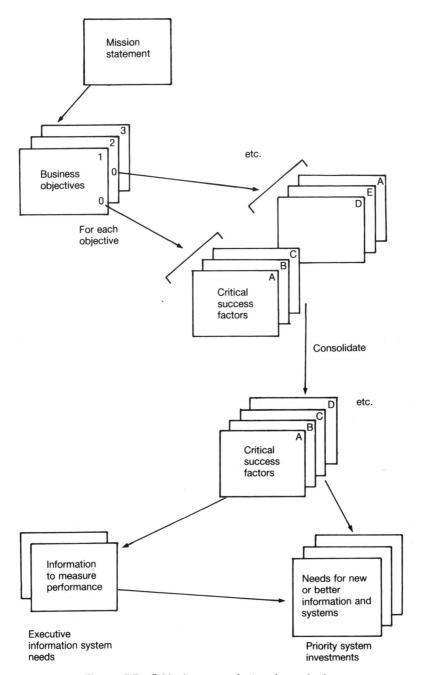

Figure 5.7 Critical success factors in context

(c) to increase sales of non-oil products in existing outlets;
(d) to reduce costs of distribution by 5 per cent; etc.

● **Critical success factors (CSFs)**: 'those things which must go right if the objectives are to be achieved' is probably the best definition. There should not be too many for each objective (normally five to eight), otherwise the objective is effectively unachievable. Certain CSFs will recur across objectives, thus giving them a heavier weighting in terms of the business dependence on their satisfactory outcome. Again following through the objectives above, CSFs for objective (a) might be:

(i) effective regional and local pricing;
(ii) increase consumers' brand awareness and loyalty;
(iii) improve non-oil product range to attract customers;
(iv) review all sites in terms of performance and productivity;
(v) ensure lead free petrol demand is matched by supplies/ pumps at outlets; etc.

The CSFs must be the product of the management's analysis of the objectives which they have set. In fact there seems little point in setting objectives unless some process like this is then undertaken to identify the key actions necessary to achieve the objectives. The CSFs introduce interim targets which are essential steps or preconditions to the achievement of longer-term goals. There is no point in reaching the year end to find an objective has not been met and then having an inquisition into the causes.

Having established the CSFs, then actions to deal with them and responsibility for those actions have to be established. For some CSFs information and systems actions will have no relevance. However, for many, improved information to monitor performance of key indicators which measure the achievement or otherwise of success factors and objectives, will at least be required. Surely if something is critical to success the top management will require regular feedback on progress towards its successful achievement? This would be the key component of any executive information system (EIS) which may well need a new method of information capture and analysis, and hence an IS investment. Many CSFs may also require improvements to be made to existing systems or even new systems to be developed. For instance, given CSF (iii) above, it is quite likely that sales of non-oil products are not recorded and analyzed in a consistent way, if at all, and therefore a new system will be needed. The need for such systems improvements may have come about through other analysis routes or merely intuitive creative thinking. CSFs are a valuable way of assessing the relative importance of such ideas in terms of how they can contribute to business success as defined by the objectives, in addition to stimulating new ideas.

Once defined, CSFs may be allocated to the various activities or combinations of activities in the business and hence in conjunction with the other techniques can help to focus IS attention – a high cost activity in the internal value chain which adds considerable value and has many CSFs is more critical for IS to address effectively than low cost, low value added, CSF free activities. In large organizations there

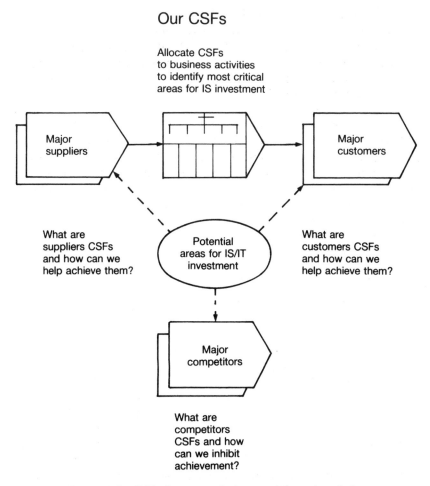

Figure 5.8 Critical success factors and the value chain

can be a cascading relationship between objectives and CSFs. Corporate objectives will have certain related CSFs, which may in turn be the source of some business unit objectives, which produce CSFs which drive functional and departmental objectives.

This analysis technique is essentially inward looking and has a short-term focus. It can be adapted to have a more creative, external value by considering the likely CSFs of major customers, suppliers and key competitors – i.e. other parties in the value chain as shown in Figure 5.8.

The CSF analysis technique is not aimed primarily at IS opportunity assessment – it is a general business strategy tool. However, it has been used extensively by companies and consultants to elicit the key areas for IS/IT investment. It is a way of achieving a consensus view of the management as to where the most beneficial IS/IT investments are to be made. It enables IS/IT potential investments to be evaluated on more than a financial contribution basis, namely by how they will affect the achievement of objectives. Hence priorities can be set and resources allocated by management judgement, and not the technician's preferences. Equally importantly, this approach can help to select the key information requirements of the senior management, i.e. executive information needs, remembering that it is always better to have a crude measure of something important than an accurate measure of something that does not matter.

Since it is important to achieve consensus throughout, the process must be managed carefully. Before embarking on CSF analysis the mission and objectives must be set by senior management and understood throughout the organization – vague or misunderstood objectives will lead to imprecise, confused success factors. Once this is done, it is best that CSFs are established by a group process involving key managers, rather than separate interviews, from which the real business CSFs are identified and then later agreed. Once agreement on CSFs is reached the potential IS opportunities for each CSF should be considered, again in a group brainstorming session, with the help of the IT management. The main risk at this stage is that each option is overevaluated by the group, rather than allocated to someone with a more detailed knowledge of the area or activities affected to evaluate its feasibility and report back later. Again the CSFs and related IS options and priorities must be understood and endorsed by the senior management team, and communicated to all those whose actions will affect their achievement.

As the business objectives change over time, so will the CSFs, and hence information systems needs and priorities. Therefore, it is important that the analysis is revisited regularly by management and that the existing priorities are reconsidered if any of the CSFs change for any reason. This provides management with a way of reviewing the IS/IT strategy from a business perspective and the means by which they can stay sensibly involved in IS/IT decision making.

Summary

As was argued in the previous chapter the appropriate level at which to establish the IS requirements (or demand) for an organization is the business unit. The framework and tools described in this chapter are used most appropriately to identify the information and systems requirements and opportunities or threats at that level. They provide the means by which management can assess the IS/IT implications of their business situation and strategy. The result is a portfolio of requirements and priorities plus an understanding of the value of existing applications. No one tool or technique will help in identifying all the requirements and no technique is a substitute for knowledge of the business or astute creative thinking. However, each of the tools can enable individuals' knowledge to be applied and focused on the role systems can play in business success. By assessing the requirements from a number of viewpoints and with a number of techniques, the most important can be confirmed and the chances of missing important options are reduced. All the techniques can be used by line management and IT specialists in concert.

Most organizations consist of more than one business unit. In terms of information systems, the business units are likely to be at different stages of development, but each could no doubt benefit from the exchange of knowledge, and the corporation itself will benefit from finding the most effective and economic means of supply. By using a common framework and applying similar analytical tools, that understanding can be transferred more coherenly from one part of the business to another. Where there are clear potential advantages from synergy – where companies trade with one another, deal with similar suppliers and customers, have similar processes or products etc. – then the use of the same rational approach to requirements determination will yield more benefits in relating the business needs. One key feature of the process described, is the need to consider what others in the industry are doing, why they are doing it, and any consequent impact. Such knowledge can be considered usefully from one industry to another, for instance, what has happened in the use of EDI in the car industry may have implications for how EDI develops in the domestic appliance industry.

One last point worth reiterating is that however the plan for systems investments (the demand) is arrived at, it must represent the agreed consensus view of all the senior and major functional managers as well as the IT department. If it does not, it will never be implemented successfully. If the plan has been established by a business driven, structured, participative approach (as proposed here) that consensus is more likely to be achieved.

Having identified the future requirements, i.e. what needs to be done, the other major IS/IT issue is how best to satisfy that demand, i.e. the supply strategy. The next chapter considers how the supply alternatives can be considered in the context of the potential portfolio of applications and business needs.

6

Creating an environment for success

Introduction

Chapters 4 and 5 considered the integration of IS/IT strategy with business strategy and establishing the business requirements for information systems. The IS/IT strategy must also resolve how these demands can be met and how the supply should be managed. All of the requirements cannot be met by one approach, but the variety of approaches adopted must be co-ordinated effectively and provide an environment within which all the requirements can be satisfied. As requirements develop and change over time, the means of supply will also have to evolve to ensure that the appropriate approach continues to be applied to the development and management of each application, the information resource, and the technology used. It is the business management's responsibility to ensure that the supply environment is developed to meet the future needs.

The requirements can be considered as a portfolio of IS applications, some of which exist already, some that are required in the short term, and others which are potential developments. The contents of the portfolio will evolve over time, but it is important that each application in the portfolio, and the portfolio overall, is managed in order to maximize the business contribution within the resources available. Hence the IS application portfolio is like other business portfolios – products, customers, investments, etc. – and each application must be understood and then managed according to its current and future business value.

A means of analyzing the application portfolio will be outlined, so that appropriate supply side strategies can be developed. Based on the key issues associated with the different types of application and their expected business contribution, appropriate management strategies are described. These strategies are based on a combined understanding of how IS/IT resources can be best deployed and also lessons from managing other business portfolios. They provide a framework for improving the contribution of existing systems, allocating resources and ensuring that the best approaches are adopted for new applications.

From this high level management overview a number of key issues will be examined in more depth. While a simple model cannot deal with all the IS/IT management issues, it can provide considerable insight into many and enable management to make informed and consistent judgements on how best to satisfy the demands.

Application portfolio analysis

There are many ways of classifying information systems, most of which are based on how they are provided, rather than the role they play in the business and the contribution they make to business success. This latter view can be achieved by considering the portfolio of applications derived from a classification originally developed by McFarlan for comparing the role of IS/IT between different organizations (see References, p.170). This version is of more value since it enables an organization to analyze its mix of existing, planned and potential systems in terms of current and future contribution and hence manage each accordingly. The classification allows each application or system to be considered in one of four segments of the portfolio matrix. The value of the application or system, as perceived by the business management, will decide whether it is one of the following:

1. High potential (turnaround).

2. Strategic.

3. Factory (key operational).

4. Support.

These terms are defined in Figure 6.1. The matrix can be used by

Strategic	High potential or turnaround
Applications which are critical to achieving future business strategy	Applications which may be important in achieving future success
Applications on which the organization currently depends for success	Applications which are valuable but not critical to business success
Factory or key operational	Support

Figure 6.1   The information systems application portfolio

senior management, users and line managers, and IS professionals, to achieve a consensus view of the contents and implications of the portfolio.

Strategic	High potential *(Turnaround)*
● Order management** ● Links to suppliers? ● MRP II** ● Sales forecasts and market analysis? ● Product profitability analysis**	● EDI with wholesalers? ● Manpower planning? ● Decision support for capacity planning? ● Expert fault diagnostics?
● Bill of materials DB* ● Inventory management* ● Shopfloor control* ● Product costing? ● Maintenance scheduling** ● Employee database** ● Receivables/payables systems* ● CAD for product design* etc.	● Time recording* ● Budgetary control* ● Expense reporting* ● General accounts* ● Maintenance costing* ● CAD for layout design? ● Payroll* ● Employee records* ● Asset register* ● Word processing* ● Electronic mail? etc.
Factory/key operational	**Support**

Figure 6.2   Example portfolio for a manufacturing company

Figure 6.2 shows a typical example matrix for a manufacturing company. The keys to the analysis are as follows:

```
*    existing system
**   planned system
?    potential system
```

The techniques described in the previous chapter are aimed at identifying the potential strategic opportunities and how the existing applications can be improved to enable that potential to be realized. To do this each existing system's value must be assessed in more detail, as the basis for further action to build on existing strengths and overcome weaknesses. For example, any application could be assessed in one or more of the following ways:

- High future potential, currently underexploited.

- Can be extended/enhanced to be of more value.

- Would be more valuable if integrated more effectively or used more extensively.

- Critical to the business but data quality is poor.

- Needs to be redeveloped to meet changed business requirements for future.

- System required but needs to be reimplemented to absorb fewer resources or overcome technology obsolescence.

- System will be less important in future, therefore needs to be simplified/reduced to real needs.

- System is no longer of value, therefore should be discontinued.

Based on such an assessment, a plan for each existing application can be developed in the light of its required business contribution.

In addition, it is important to understand where resources and funds are currently being used and are planned to be used across the matrix, to identify whether resource levels need to be changed or resources redeployed. Most companies need to move resources to more *strategic* applications but not neglect *factory* systems, if business objectives are to be achieved. This implies that unless total resources are increased the resources used for *support* systems must be reduced. This could just mean a substitution of funds for scarce people skills, to buy in support systems, packages or external services, or a real reduction in investment, if funds as well as skilled staff are not available.

This application portfolio matrix has many similarities with the better known product portfolio matrix (or Boston Square), which is useful in deciding how to develop the different components of the business and allocate resources. Valuable ideas derived from the Boston Square, such as life cycle management, can be transferred to the application portfolio to assist management judgement.

Before considering management strategies for supplying the systems it is important to understand the main reasons or <u>driving forces</u> for the types of application and hence some of the resulting issues to be managed. Some of the key factors which have to be considered for the applications in the different segments are as follows:

1. **High potential (turnaround) applications:**
    The driving forces behind the applications are often:

    (a) a new business idea or technological opportunity;
    (b) an individual initiative in one part of the business, the idea being owned by someone who champions it;
    (c) the objective which is to demonstrate the value, and then decide whether and how to exploit it for business benefit.

    Hence the requirements will normally be:

    (a) the rapid evaluation of prototypes, with an ability to reject failures, before they waste resources;
    (b) to understand the potential of the application in relation to the business strategy and the likely economics of further investment;
    (c) to identify the best way to proceed – what to do next, how that should be done and by whom.

    The basic philosophy is R&D – namely controlled experimentation to identify the potential benefits, opportunities and costs etc. involved – then to decide if further investment is worthwhile (or not) and how the next stage of the application development should be managed. For example, in Figure 6.2 the potential electronic data interchange (EDI) links to wholesalers needs to be evaluated not just by the company but also by the wholesalers on whose co-operation it will depend if any business benefits are to be achieved.

2. **Strategic applications:**
    The driving forces are likely to be:

(a) market requirements and/or competitive pressures, essentially externally driven (perhaps by suppliers or customers);

(b) business objectives, success factors and management vision of how to achieve them;

(c) obtaining an advantage and then sustaining it by further developments if possible.

Hence some requirements are:

(a) rapid development to meet the business objective, and realize the business benefits within the window of opportunity;

(b) a flexible solution which can be adapted further to meet changes in the business environment;

(c) links to an associated business initiative or change to sustain the business commitment to the IS/IT development.

The overriding approach is business driven – driven by the business imperatives to which the ideal IT approach must, if necessary, be compromised. The prime risk is missing a business opportunity which will undoubtedly be time dependent, and a critical facet is managing business change. To be considered as strategic, any application must be related clearly to the critical success factors derived from business objectives. Again in Figure 6.2, comprehensive order management to satisfy service needs expressed by customers may well become a competitive weapon, that is if competitors cannot provide similar responses to the same customers. However, these needs will probably change over time and vary from customer to customer.

3. **Factory (key operational) applications**:
   The driving forces are normally:

   (a) improving the performance of existing activities, in terms of speed, accuracy, effectiveness and economics;

   (b) integrating systems and data to avoid misinformation and duplication of tasks, to minimize the risk of activities being inconsistently or ineffectively performed;

   (c) avoiding a business disadvantage or preventing a business risk from becoming critical.

   Hence some requirements will be:

   (a) high quality (long life) solutions and effective data management, to ensure a degree of stability and reduced costs of change over time;

   (b) balancing costs with benefits and business risks, to identify the best solution to the business problem;

(c) the evaluation of options available to select the most effective, by means of an objective analysis of the feasible alternatives.

This is the traditional IS/IT domain for which tools and methodologies have been developed over the last thirty years and the best IS/IT approaches, derived from years of experience, should not be compromised for business expediency. In Figure 6.2 a sound product costing system which links to the bill of materials database and inventory management is essential if product profitability analysis is to be carried out. Its integration with existing systems is critical to achieve consistency and accuracy.

4. **Support applications**:
    Driving forces are often:
    (a) improved productivity and efficiency of specific (often localized) existing tasks;
    (b) legal requirements, which have to be met to avoid prosecution;
    (c) most cost effective use of IS/IT funds and resources, to find the most business efficient solution.

    Hence the requirements become:
    (a) lowest cost, long-term solutions which often lead to package software and even compromising user needs to the solutions available;
    (b) avoiding obsolescence by evolution at the pace of the IS/IT industry;
    (c) objective cost/benefit analysis to reduce financial risk, and ensure the costs of development are easily controlled.

    Here the economics of the investment will be the main reason for deciding whether to go ahead and in selecting the approach. It is also the area which is similar for most organizations and hence for which the most packaged software is available. In Figure 6.2 the maintenance costing system was deemed to be out of date and inefficient, but since it is not considered critical, its re-development would be an economic decision. It is likely that a proprietary package would be the most economic way of meeting the needs.

Clearly the issues to be managed in each segment of the matrix are different, as are the risks of failure of the systems as well as the potential benefits. Therefore, different strategies are needed to manage them.

Generic IS/IT management strategies

Based on extensive observation of the realities of IS/IT management in many organizations Parsons describes six strategies as the means by which organizations link the management of IS/IT to the business management processes. His strategies (called 'generic strategies' hereafter) are 'general frameworks which guide the opportunities for IT which are identified, the IT resources which are developed, the rate at which new technologies are adopted, the level of impact for IT within the firm, etc.'. The six strategies described are 'the central tendencies which firms use to guide IT within the business', hence the adoption of the word 'generic' since this definition is similar to the concept of generic business strategies of low cost and differentiation (see References, p.170).

Generic strategies are ways of succeeding in the management of IS/IT in the long term, provided the appropriate strategy or mix of strategies is adopted for a given set of circumstances. The characteristics and implications of each strategy are described in detail in Table 6.1. Those characteristics and implications are summarized here sufficient for an understanding of each strategy and the differences between them. How they can be employed as part of the IS/IT management process is then considered.

The six strategies are as follows:

1. Centrally planned.

2. Leading edge.

3. Free market.

4. Monopoly.

5. Scarce resource.

6. Necessary evil.

They are well titled since the very names evoke a basic understanding of the attitudes and behaviour that each is likely to produce. The key points of each, and their pros and cons, will be outlined before considering their implications.

1. **Centrally planned**:

    (a) IS/IT strategy is totally integrated with corporate strategy through a centralized, senior, dedicated agency;

Table 6.1 The generic strategies (after Parsons)

	Centrally planned	Leading edge	Free market	Monopoly	Scarce resources	Necessary evil
Requires	• Knowledgeable and involved senior management • A mechanism for planning IS/IT within the business planning process process	• Commitment of funds and resources • Innovative IS/IT management • Strong technical skills	• Knowledgeable users • Accountability for IS/IT at business or functional level • Willingness to duplicate effort • Loose IT budget control	• User acceptance of the philosophy • Policies to force through single sourcing • Good forecasting of resource usage	• Tight budgetary control of all IS/IT expenses • Policies for controlling IS/IT and users	• Very tight IT control • Meet basic needs only
Management logic	• Central co-ordination of all requirements will produce better decision making	• Technology can create business advantages and risks are worth taking	• Market makes the best decisions and users are responsible for business results • Integration is not critical	• Information is a corporate good and an integrated resource for users to employ	• Information is limited resource and its development must be clearly justified	• Information is not important to business
Internal IS role	• Provide services to match the business demands by linking closely with business managers	• Push forward boundaries of technology use on all fronts	• Competitive and probably profit centre intended to achieve a return on its resources	• To satisfy users' requirements as they arise but non-directive in terms of the uses of IS/IT	• Make best use of a limited resource by tight cost control of expenses and projects. Justify capital investment projects	• Maintain minimum resources and skill levels • Respond to well justified needs only by return on investment (ROI)
Users' role	• Identify the potential of IS/IT to meet business needs at all levels of the organization	• Use the technology and identify the advantages it offers	• Identify, source and control IS/IT developments	• Understand needs and present them to central utility to obtain resources, etc.	• Identify and cost justify projects • Passive unless benefits are identified	• Very passive and no role in the IS/IT resource development

(b) this enables understanding of competitive opportunities and requirements, resources to be deployed optimally and large investments to be undertaken, especially those which span a number of proposed applications.

The strategy is very demanding of senior management time and can be difficult to make effective in many organizations. It can also become removed from 'sharp end' business realities and may inhibit innovation.

2. **Leading edge**:

   (a) implies an intrinsic acceptance that IT will create competitive advantage and hence 'state-of-the-art' technology must be sustained;
   (b) involves R&D expenditure and often many wasted investments, and requires senior management commitment to the concept, if not heavy involvement.

   It can be expensive and requires adept management to convert entrepreneurial ideas into effective applications. It is not a strategy which can be adopted for all applications, but is required if technology developments are to be exploited. 'Leading edge' implies relative to IS/IT use in the particular industry.

3. **Free market**:

   (a) implies that user management knows what is best for the business, including IS/IT, and can therefore assess its own requirements and satisfy them as wished;
   (b) internal IT services must compete with outside vendors and can expect little attention from senior management.

   It can cause duplication of investment and differential rates of development across the organization, but will lead to business/ user driven innovation in IS/IT usage. It is not a strategy which produces integration of systems. A true free market implies that if users can choose how to resource their applications, the IT group must be allowed to sell its services outside the organization.

4. **Monopoly**:

   (a) IS/IT is provided by a sole source utility or service within the organization, to which all users have to make requests;
   (b) user satisfaction with services provided is the main measure of its effectiveness;
   (c) the overall expenditure on IS/IT is easy to identify, and hence control.

It can mean innovation is slow and perhaps unable to respond to competitive needs, since the users do not perceive IS in that role. However, a well run monopoly will provide a very professional service in terms of systems' quality. The ability to satisfy all user demands implies having excess capacity to respond to urgent needs. The existence of an application backlog implies a failure to satisfy user requirements.

5. **Scarce resource**:
   (a) a budget is set in advance and applications compete for a share of the resource available;
   (b) a very popular strategy which ensures careful management of IT resources using financial controls;
   (c) investments must be well justified in financial terms, and a tendency to focus on the returns on investment in setting priorities prevails.

   Given management's view that IS/IT is a cost centre and the objective is its controlled, well justified use, it is not conducive to it being exploited or speculated with as a business weapon. The strategy does not recognize changes in demand, and priority setting will be a major issue in the planning process.

6. **Necessary evil**:
   A strategy of only deploying IS/IT to meet legal requirements and for very high return investments, i.e. using IS/IT <u>only where no other alternative is available</u>.

   The strategy has many disadvantages, unless IS/IT is almost entirely irrelevant to the business, or the business itself is being treated as a low priority for investments of any type. A necessary evil strategy normally occurs by mistake or neglect, perhaps due to overzealous scarce resourcing. Symptoms of such a situation are high staff turnover and very defensive IT managers unable and unwilling to take any risks. Demoralization then leads to a lack of capability. Such situations can, however, be observed in some companies in many industries. Once such a situation exists it is very difficult to get out of, and involves not just expenditure but often completely new IT management.

In practical terms these strategies as described above have certain key differences, some of which are more obvious than others (see also Table 6.1).

Central planning and monopoly have certain similarities but central planning is essentially a demand management strategy by which the business and IT managers together plan the best route to achieving all the main demands for applications. Monopoly is a supply management strategy – controlling the supply of technology and resources, not funds, to satisfy the evolving user needs. It does not mean that the IT group does all the work, but it gives permission for users to solve problems within the preferred supply strategy. Scarce resourcing is a financial management strategy which asks users and IT to explain the value of investments in financial terms. It is not the negative attitude to IS/IT that necessary evil implies. Free market and leading edge are strategies for innovation, the former led by business demands, the latter driven by technological developments. These strategies can be seen as an evolution of how IS/IT is managed as its contribution to the business increases over time.

In the early days of IS/IT either individual departments began to develop systems independently and/or the investments were justified by return on investment (ROI), offsetting the capital and development costs against calculated efficiency benefits. As investments increased resources were often centralized to achieve economies of scale, integration and higher quality of results in the long term. Large monopolies, however, became constrictive, backlogs built up and users became frustrated with the limited supply options available. By the early 1980s personal computers enabled users to overcome some of these constraints and to seek their own solutions. Often this caused a major rift between the monopolistic centre and the newly liberated users. At about the same time senior management attitudes to funding the ever increasing IS/IT cost centre, initiated attempts to improve its contribution by forcing a profit centre motivation, deliberately forcing a free market. The response of many previously inert IS/IT monopolies to market pressure was to extend their technology base into new technologies which previously had been resisted. As the full understanding of strategic IS/IT potential arrived in organizations, processes of central planning were developed to enable links to be made with business strategy.

That may be an oversimplified description of events, but the behaviour of many companies is typical of the trends. After initial haphazard beginnings to computing, it was often centralized under the financial function, often the main user and the scarce resourcing strategy is a natural consequence of financial control of IS/IT. Many organizations still have IS/IT as part of finance. Most major corporations set up monopolistic style utilities in the 1960s and 1970s to provision the business with IS/IT. Many of these were restrictive monopolies and still are. Many companies, such as British Leyland (ISTEL), Imperial Metals (IMI), Debenhams and BTR evolved to free markets in the late 1970s and early 1980s setting up independent IS/IT companies. This trend has been followed by many others, including local government bodies and health authorities, in the 1980s. Some have found problems with this approach as the IS/IT company succeeds, develops strategic applications and then seeks a market (potentially competitors) in which to profit from those developments. Major United Kingdom retailers in the 1980s have developed central planning mechanisms to enable major point-of-sale and network investments to be managed effectively. Financial service companies have been less successful with attempts to achieve central planning as products and services begin to integrate. Banks with a long history of devolved IS/IT strategies are finding more problems than building societies who have been less IS/IT dependent historically and also have a more centralized culture. However, as the building societies expand their business following deregulation into estate agency, insurance, banking, etc., the central planning approach is becoming strained. One significant observation is that once a free market strategy dominates it is very difficult to convert to any other – it is very expensive to 'buy out'.

It is at this level of dominating strategies that Parsons describes the implications pointing out, for instance, how a scarce resource strategy will seriously inhibit the development of strategic applications because of the following:

1. Business strategy is not known or understood by users making requests.

2. Business strategy is unknown to the (IT) group doing systems work.

3. Strategic benefits are hard to quantify.

He argues similarly with regard to each strategy, but as he points out, historically at least, management has generally adopted one approach to managing IS/IT, implying that one generic strategy is prevalent. Given a limited portfolio of applications this may at some point in the past have been sufficient if not ideal. He then examines how each strategy fits onto the applications portfolio in order to identify the best approach available to the systems in each segment of the portfolio. He concludes that in each case one or two strategies will work best. It is from this simple and logical correlation that the

Strategic	High potential	
Centrally planned	Leading edge Free market	Demand
Monopoly	Scarce resource Free market (Necessary evil)	Supply
Factory/key operational	Support	

←———Centralized   Decentralized ———→

Figure 6.3 Viable generic strategies related to strategic importance of systems

generic strategies become useful in establishing appropriate IS/IT management processes.

The overlay of ideal generic strategies on the portfolio model is depicted in Figure 6.3. Central planning is a demand management strategy driven by the business needs whereas monopoly is mainly a supply management approach and both imply centralization of decision making. Leading edge is a demand management approach driven by technology. Scarce resource is obviously a supply management strategy based on limiting the supply of money. Free market can be both, allowing users to determine demand and/or decide on the source of supply.

Given the different driving forces and requirements for the applications in each segment the strategies can be seen to be appropriate. The strategic and high potential segments are about seeking opportunities, identifying future advantages and then managing these new demands successfully. In the factory and support segments the focus on resolving current business problems, taking opportunities as they arise, and hence careful management to reduce risk and disadvantage is essential.

Overplanning of high potential applications can stifle innovation – the two strategies which will fit best are leading edge and free market, both of which are risky but will cause innovation. Key issues in this segment are concerned with evaluating opportunities and pursuing innovative ideas to success. There are inherent risks and hence the objective is to identify the best way of obtaining the business benefits of the application of technology. Strategic applications require the central planning approach to ensure the business drive determines what the system does and how it is done, to resolve the level of risk that is worth taking to achieve the benefits. The systems will succeed by close integration with the particular business needs, not just in terms of what is done but also when it is delivered. A monopoly strategy, while potentially restrictive, is ideal to reduce risks, providing quality solutions over the long term, a requirement for factory systems. The highly centralized and controlled approach enables critical issues of integration of systems and information to be resolved so that all business needs are met in the most effective way without risk of failure. A very structured approach is essential. Scarce resourcing is ideal in controlling support systems investments, requiring a clear statement of the expected outcome before allocating resources. Equally, the free market can be used on the basis of user discretion to spend their own funds – since integration will not normally be a critical issue, it is more important to obtain, process and use the information in the most efficient way. This implies reducing risk by a steady evolution with careful user and/or financial control.

Using generic strategies in developing the environment for success

The generic strategies have primarily two uses in the process of developing the appropriate IS/IT management approaches, as follows:

1. **Diagnostic**: they are a way of assessing the current situation and of understanding and expressing the ways in which IS/IT is being managed. There is a strong correlation between the applications developed and the strategies adopted – a cause and effect relationship. The generic strategies can encapsulate the apparent complexity of the existing situation, explain it and describe it succinctly.

2. **Formulative**: once a future portfolio of applications can be identified and the strengths and weaknesses of the existing applications assessed, the generic strategies can be used to identify a migration path towards the required future mix. It is superficially attractive to say central planning is needed, but it might be an overkill and it is impossible to plan everything centrally. Allowing more freedom, using new technology or tighter, monopolistic control

may be more appropriate in the short term. More rigorous scarce resourcing of support systems might yield resources to be deployed on strategic systems.

No mixture can be prescribed for every situation but the generic strategies provide a limited number of basic options from which to select an appropriate set which matches the application portfolio requirements. This approach avoids the need to invent the strategy entirely from the ground up – it is easier to define the strategic approach by modification from proven approaches to suit the particular need and then identify the action necessary to achieve the migration path.

The application portfolio in a multiple business unit organization

The analysis of applications into the four components of the matrix is carried out most appropriately for a business unit. Indeed each business unit should assess the IS/IT contribution in such terms and hence determine how IS/IT can best be managed to achieve success. In a multibusiness unit organization there then occurs another level of management of IS/IT.

In a diversified conglomerate evolving through acquisition and divestment of business units the corporate IS/IT generic strategies are likely to consist of a minimal centralized component – perhaps financial control systems – with an otherwise free market philosophy. This is appropriate to the organization. However, if the company is predominantly in one industry where synergy is a potential source of advantage, the business unit strategies are likely to be supplemented at a corporate level by some central planning of related IS/IT applications and perhaps a monopolistic control over the ways of meeting key operational needs in order to avoid proliferation and incompatibility of solutions. Where the organization cannot benefit from vertical synergy, but consists of like types of companies (e.g. manufacturing, or retail, or financial services), similarity of functional requirements might be satisfied more effectively or economically from a central utility (monopoly) for those systems which are needed by many companies. The application portfolio concept enables the matrix of approaches to be adopted to satisfy the individual business unit and to take advantage of similarities of need and economic routes to common solutions. For each corporate situation a suitably structured mixture can be arrived at.

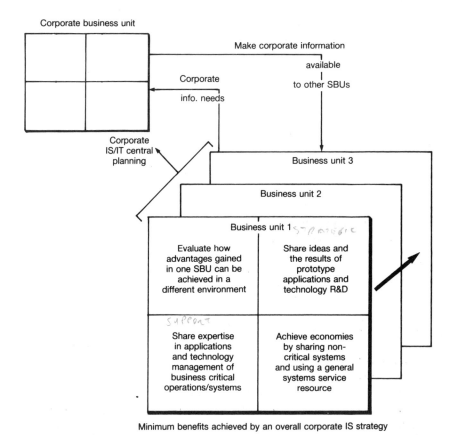

Figure 6.4   Portfolio management in a multiple strategic business unit (multi-SBU) organization

Figure 6.4 depicts the minimum gains to be made by a co-ordinated approach across the organization. In the support box, even if the businesses are diverse, the applications are likely to address similar administrative requirements and packages are a common choice. At worst a limited number of packages should be used, at best a common suite of applications could be used. This will depend on the diversity of the business. Manufacturing and financial services will require different systems, but several types of retail company in different market sectors could easily use common accounting systems, etc. The same logic applies throughout the matrix but the areas of potential commonality of actual applications is likely to decrease as we progress from support to factory to strategic, although the potential in the last box may be realizable through different uses of the same idea. Providing similar technological environments in the different units even if the businesses are different (say leisure and retail) may enable supply-based expertise to provide better quality factory solutions to both. Sharing the advantages gained from one organization to another may accelerate the development of strategic applications – this implies business-based sharing of how to achieve the benefits available, even if the details of the applications vary. Links to suppliers for instance are likely to achieve similar benefits to manufacturing and retail companies. All this will require a corporate view of the portfolios of the various units so that concepts of generic strategies can be extrapolated to a higher level – not to drive the strategies but to ensure opportunities are not missed or resources and funds needlessly wasted.

Issues in managing the application portfolio

The previous discussion considered how the application portfolio can be used to match the demand for information systems with the appropriate way of managing the supply. This is a high level view which needs to be considered in more detail when it comes to developing and managing particular applications. From all that has been said before it is obvious that systems in the various segments are driven by different issues and need different approaches to many aspects of their development and management. The role of systems will also evolve over time and they will need to be managed across segment boundaries: from high potential to strategic, as the potential is to be realized; from strategic to factory as the comparative advantage is negated and the system becomes more stable and disadvantage is to be avoided. High potential opportunities may only produce limited support type local benefits, factory systems can become less critical as the business evolves and may move into support mode. Finally some applications, mainly support systems, will become obsolete and will need to be removed.

This evolution of systems over time shows one of the similarities of this portfolio with product portfolios in which products over time move through a life cycle, if successful, from wild cat via star to cash cow to become dogs before being removed from the portfolio. During each stage the product needs to be managed differently, success factors will change and more or less resources will be worth investing

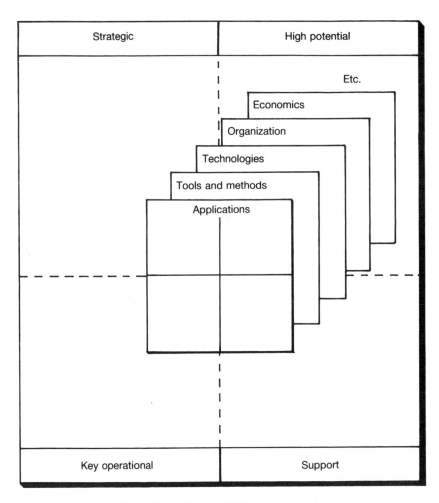

Figure 6.5 Portfolio analysis – IS/IT management dimensions

according to its current and expected future contribution. Other lessons can be drawn from managing an evolving product portfolio whose success is dependent on both external and internal business factors, as is the case with the applications portfolio. This is especially true in a competitive environment, where the systems investments of others can change the relevance and importance of the organization's portfolio. Figure 6.5 identifies a number of the aspects of IS development and management which are affected by the differing requirements and issues to be resolved. This also implies a transition from one approach to another when due to its business role changing, a system moves between segments. Most systems have been managed in the same way for many years although their importance to the business has changed significantly. This usually results in excessive use of resources to achieve ever diminishing benefits or a failure of the system to meet the current business needs effectively.

A number of the more detailed aspects of methods and techniques to be used in delivering the systems and the technologies to be adopted are covered in the next chapter. These lead to a definition of the skills and types of resources required and how these are to be developed or procured and then organized most effectively. These aspects are addressed in Chapter 8 within the framework established in this chapter.

One key aspect which deserves more specific attention is the evaluation and justification of IS/IT investments in the different segments, and how priorities are established across the matrix, given that it will be impossible to do everything immediately. It must be remembered that IS/IT investments compete with other business investments such as plant, buildings, stock, marketing, etc., for the organization's funds, as well as with each other for funds and limited skilled resources. Therefore they must be evaluated in a way that allows comparison with other business investments and also across contending applications. Such an approach must be applied consistently, and hence be a clearly understood policy within which proposals can be compared. Also it is important that whatever policy is established for evaluating and justifying investments it should be the basis for setting priorities for resource and fund allocation, otherwise the resulting plans will not be aimed at delivering the maximum overall benefit from the resources available.

In all cases the costs expected to be incurred and the resources needed, must be estimated as accurately as possible – though this will obviously be easier on support and factory applications where experience is greater than for strategic and high potential applications where there will be considerable uncertainty. The estimates must take a realistic view of long-term costs over the expected life of the system. Most evaluation processes are conservative and rarely allow for the rapidly reducing costs of some components of a system. Raw IT costs have been decreasing steadily by some 20–25 per cent per annum over many years, whereas in general labour and software costs are increasing. All evaluations should be based on real costs not any internal transfer prices which are used for allocating IS/IT costs to users. These are subject to usage, activity levels and productivity variances, and are an unreliable basis for business evaluation. The costs should also include those to be incurred in the user departments. Identifying and quantifying the expected benefits of any system can be very difficult and often can only be assessed with any accuracy once the system is installed. However, it is important to define the target benefits, quantify and express financially those that can be. Again, this should be easier for support and factory systems than for strategic and high potential applications.

Evaluating IS/IT investments

In the book *Information Economics*, Parker *et al.* (1988) assess in detail the ways in which IS benefits really accrue and how they can be quantified to help in justifying investments. They consider three main types of application in terms of the benefits expected as follows:

1. **Substitutive**: machine power for people power – economics being the main driving force to improve efficiency.

2. **Complementary**: improving productivity and employee effectiveness by enabling work to be performed in new ways.

3. **Innovative**: intended to obtain or sustain competitive edge by changing trading practice or creating new markets, etc.

These three types of application benefit can be translated into the terms of the portfolio as follows:

1. Substitutive relates mainly to support and factory systems.

2. Complementary relates primarily to factory and strategic segments.

3. Innovative imply mainly strategic and high potential applications.

Parker *et al.* then identify the ways in which applications should be justified and define five basic techniques for evaluating benefits, as follows:

1. The traditional cost/benefit analysis, based on cost displacement by a more efficient way of carrying out a task. For example, preparing invoices by computer and transmitting them electronically by means of a data network is more efficient than printing and posting them, both for the sender and receiver.

2. Value linking, which estimates the improvement to business performance, not just savings made, by more precise co-ordination of tasks in different areas – being able to bill customers more accurately, due to immediate delivery feedback, or satisfy a greater proportion of customer orders direct from stock due to the precision of the stock records, are examples of value linking.

3. Value acceleration, which considers the time dependency of benefits and costs in other departments, of system improvements – for example, being able to prepare invoices one day earlier or giving sales data to buyers sooner, giving them more time to negotiate with suppliers. This implies that the benefit will occur in another area of the business.

4. Value restructuring, which considers the productivity resulting from organizational change and change of job roles, enabled by the new system. For instance departments can be combined, even eliminated due to systems developed to carry out functions in an integrated fashion. Information intensive tasks such as forecasting, planning and scheduling can often be rationalized and improved.

5. Innovation evaluation attempts to identify the value of new business or new business practices levered from IS/IT. The value may be in the application itself, for example, the use of expert systems to diagnose machine faults, or in the image it creates for the company (for instance, home banking services).

Table 6.2 shows how the emphasis of the techniques of benefit evaluation can be expected to align to the different segments of the portfolio. The number of asterisks identifies the degree to which the benefit type is likely to fit the application type. Each of the segments is now considered in more detail, in terms of the investment rationale.

Table 6.2   Types of benefit expected by types of application

	High potential	Strategic	Factory	Support
1. Cost benefit analysis	–	*	***	****
2. Value linking	*	**	****	***
3. Value acceleration	**	***	***	***
4. Value restructuring	**	****	**	*
5. Innovation	****	****	*	–

* Number of asterisks identifies degrees of relevance.

Support applications
The main argument for such systems is improving efficiency, which should be possible to quantify and convert into a financial argument for investment. If the application development requires the use of scarce (central) resources, it is reasonable to expect potential benefits to be estimated before resources and costs are incurred, to identify the most economic solution within the benefits achievable. If the application is competing with others for the limited resource, then a support application must show a good economic return for the allocation of a scarce resource. If, however, the project can be carried out within the user department's control, then it is reasonable that, since the budget or funding is under local control, the go/no go decision is made by local user management. The IS/IT investment is an alternative use of funds to other investments locally and is not competing with alternative use of scarce IS/IT resources. Hopefully user management will expect the case to be argued in predominantly financial terms, but if not, that is the user management's responsibility.

Factory (or key operational) applications
While as far as possible all costs and benefits of a new development or redevelopment or enhancement to a factory system should be converted to a financial evaluation, this may not allow for all the arguments involved. For support systems it was suggested that benefits should be estimated before any resource is allocated or costs determined. This is inappropriate for factory applications where financial benefits are not the only driving force, and also the most economic solution may not be the most effective. This is the area for strict feasibility study to find the best solution from a range of alternatives, each with differing costs and benefits and risks.

The business success may be at risk if a system falls behind the business needs. It also might be worth spending more to achieve an integrated solution which meets a range of needs more effectively and upon which new strategic applications can be built. The relationship of the system to other existing, proposed and potential systems must be included in the evaluation. Normally this will increase the cost and the intangible benefits. Some of those benefits will be able to be related to critical success factors which will, if achieved, lead to achievement of business objectives (and vice versa if they are not). An argument often used here is 'what will happen to the business if we do not invest in improving factory systems' and therefore 'can we afford the risk of not doing it?' – will failure to invest perhaps reduce the ability to achieve future objectives?

The strategy that works best for factory systems is monopoly, which implies a central control and vetting of all applications and enhancements. This enables a standard checklist of questions to be considered in the evaluation of any new project. The monopoly approach should also preclude solutions based on only economic expediency rather than total business benefits, although it may mean that a particular application may cost more in the short term.

Strategic applications
The fact that an application is deemed strategic implies that it is essential to achieving business objectives and strategies. Obviously, it is important to cost the investment and where possible put figures to the potential benefits, even if the latter are only orders of magnitude, not estimates suitable for a discounted cash flow calculation. However, the main reasons for proceeding are likely to remain intangible, expressed as the critical success factors which the application addresses.

The strategy most appropriate for this part of the matrix is central planning, whereby IS/IT opportunities and threats are being considered along with the business issues and strategies. Hence, an application will get the go/no go decision based on whether it is relevant to the business objectives and strategy and likely to deliver benefits in those terms, not as a system in its own right. Whether this will actually happen is partly a question of luck (that the target does not move), partly of judgement (the quality of business acumen of senior managers), and partly good management of the application as and when it is developed. The key issue is whether the management team is united in endorsing the project and that the organization deems the investment worthwhile. The critical factor is then, resourcing the task sufficiently to achieve the objectives in the optimum timescale. This may need repeated senior management intervention to ensure both user and IS/IT resources are made available.

High potential applications
The very essence of high potential projects is that the benefits are unknown. The objective is to identify the potential benefits available. It is the R&D segment of the matrix and should be justified on the same basis as any other R&D project, and preferably from a general R&D budget rather than IS/IT central funds. It is important not to pour money into the seemingly bottomless pit that R&D can become if it is not monitored properly. The idea of product champions to be responsible for such projects, given a budget against agreed general terms of reference and to deliver results or otherwise, is the most

effective way of initiating and managing the high potential stage in an application's life cycle. Evaluation is what the high potential box is really about – nothing should stay in it too long or have too much money spent on it. When initial allocations are used up, further sums have to be rejustified, not just allocated in the vague hope of eventual success. This approach fits the leading edge and free market strategies that the box needs. However, it should be obvious that those responsible for ensuring that central planning works for strategic applications should be well aware of what is being evaluated in the high potential segment, by whom and to what purpose.

The approaches to application justification in the various segments described above may lack the precision required ideally, but this is no more than is true of other aspects of R&D, advertising, reorganization, building new plant or facilities, taking on new staff or training people, i.e., other major business investments.

Setting priorities for applications

As mentioned earlier, the mechanisms used to decide whether or not applications go ahead should also be used to set priorities across applications when all cannot be done in parallel. Some priorities are logical, for instance project B cannot proceed before project A has built the database, but many more are independent of each other. Therefore, it is important to introduce some consistent, rational approach to priority setting if any plan is to be implemented successfully. Short-term business pressures will change, projects will not proceed as planned, resources will not be available as expected, new opportunities and requirements will emerge. Each of these can change the priorities and unless a consistent rationale is employed, the short-term issues will override the strategy. In that short term, resources are limited and must be used to maximum effect. The main constraint is normally skilled people, often in particular skill areas, in both user and IT communities.

From the earlier discussion of application evaluation it should be seen that setting priorities among applications in a particular segment, such as support or factory, is not too difficult. Other than ranking them on similarly expressed benefits, the remaining parameter is to optimize the resource use. It might also be prudent to modify the desired priorities by consideration of the ability to succeed – the risk of each application – to ensure that not just high risk projects are tackled, eventually resulting in no achievement. Hence, three factors need to be included in the assessment of priorities as follows:

1. What it is most important to do, i.e. benefits.

2. What is capable of being done, i.e. resources.

3. What is likely to succeed, i.e. risks.

Much research has been carried out on why projects fail, and checklists of risk factors are readily available. The main risk factors are concerned with project size and duration, business instability, organizational rate of change and the number of parts of the organization involved in the development, rather than technical factors, unless very new technology is used.

Within the support segment, setting priorities should not be too difficult – those with the greatest economic benefit that use the least resources should get the highest priority. This will encourage users to express benefits quantitatively and look for resource efficient solutions, such as packages, to obtain a priority. Within the strategic segment, the basic rationale is equally clear. Those applications which will contribute most to achieving business objectives, and use the least resources in the process, should go ahead first. To assess this, some form of simple decision table to express each project in terms of the critical success factors (CSFs) it affects can be useful in assessing the strategic contribution of different projects. It produces a strategic score, or value, for each application or project. While CSFs cannot be weighted (by definition), the business objectives can be given relative priorities. Each application should be explained in terms of how, and therefore to what degree, it will help in achieving the various success factors. Such a decision support tool should not be used mechanistically – a score of 25 is not necessarily better than 24, it means they are about equally important. Again, by dividing the score by the 'man' years of resource required, the overall contribution from the resources can be maximized.

All applications, wherever they fall in the matrix, should be assessed against such a strategic weighting table to help decide in which segment they belong. High potential applications should demonstrate some, if as yet unclear, relationship to objectives, whereas strategic applications will contribute more directly. Support systems will show little strategic contribution (otherwise they are more important), and factory applications should relate to at least some CSFs, if only in a negative or risk avoidance way.

Setting priorities among factory systems is more problematic than for support or strategic systems, where the basic rationale is simpler. The arguments for (i.e. benefits of) factory systems will comprise basically economic considerations, CSFs, risk to current business, and infrastructure improvement. Each of these issues must be given some form of relative weighting to decide order of preference before looking at resource constraints.

In each case the cost and resources used by the project should be matched against its importance in each of the four categories to establish overall priorities. Economic benefits and CSFs have already been considered. Infrastructure reflects the IT view of developing a coherent systems and data architecture, increasing skills, improving the resilience or flexibility of systems and the technology base. This will both avoid excessive cost of supporting the systems but also provide a firm foundation for strategic developments. Risk to current business could be assessed in a similar way by 'what risks do we run if the project does not go ahead?'. Applications scoring highly in all four categories are more important than those scoring highly in one, two or three categories. Those at each level in the ranking using less resources get priority. It is a subjective method but does allow the strategic, financial, user and IT perspectives to be included.

High potential applications are difficult to prioritize and will tend to be driven somewhat in the reverse of strategic applications, namely deciding what resource is available to do it and then which application might best employ that resource. If, as was suggested earlier, high potential applications are often individually driven having a keen champion, then it is the secondary resources which are the problem. While it sounds incorrect to suggest that the person 'who shouts the loudest', or 'has the most influence', will obtain priority in this segment, it may be the best way to allow priorities to be set because: the results will depend not only on the value of the idea, but also the force with which it is pursued; and setting objective priorities on scanty evidence is not very reliable anyway. If the idea potentially impacts many CSFs it clearly stands out from others and should be elevated above the general scramble for R&D type resources. In the discussion below high potential applications are not considered as being in competition for IS/IT funds, but are funded from R&D general budgets. However, they may compete for certain key skills or resources.

The remaining task is to set priorities across the segments of the portfolio to decide how much resource to devote to the different types of applications. This is not simple since the rationale for investment in each is different, as shown above. How, for example, can management compare a market analysis system which will help segment the customers more precisely, with a pallet control system for the warehouse which will save two staff? However, the approach recommended can be used to assess all types of applications. The problem is that strategic applications (such as the market analysis system) will score heavily in CSFs whereas support applications (such as pallet control) will score heavily on economics, whereas factory systems will score on risk and infrastructure. Management must decide the weighting to be attributed to each type of benefit and then rank the systems.

The relative weighting given to each will depend on a number of business and IS/IT factors such as the following:

- The strength or weakness of the business position will affect the need to defend the current position or to become more innovative.
- The strengths and weaknesses of existing systems and the capabilities of the IS/IT resource, based on previous delivery performance.
- The experience and competence of users in defining requirements and implementing systems successfully.

Another important factor will be the degree of confidence that management has in its own business judgement relative to the need to be reassured by figures. The more confidence that management has in the users and IS/IT to develop effective systems, the greater will be the weighting placed on the CSFs, etc., relative to financial aspects. This is an indication of the maturity of the organization in how it plans and manages IS/IT. It also tends to reflect the strength of the company within its industry.

If the overall plan is developed and maintained in a priority sequence that reflects the following ratio:

$$\frac{\text{Benefits to be achieved (adjusted for risk)}}{\text{Limiting resource consumed}}$$

then it helps both in short- and long-term planning decisions because: resources can be allocated where necessary from lower to higher priority applications on a rational basis, with the agreement of users; and appropriate resourcing levels for the future can be set, and action taken to obtain the right type of resources to meet the demands. It is important to communicate the resulting plan to all involved so as to aid understanding of the reasons for the ranking of any particular project. Mystery or uncertainty are far more destructive of strategies than the discussion and reconciliation of real problems.

Again the above arguments may lack the precision ideally required for setting priorities, but given that rules for the various factors involved can be established sensibly, it is better than each priority decision being made on a different set of criteria.

In both the evaluation of projects and setting priorities, the one aspect which must not be ignored is 'after the event'. Some form of review/audit (but not a witch hunt) must be carried out on a high percentage of projects to identify whether they were carried out as well as possible, and whether the benefits claimed (and possibly different benefits) were achieved or not. A factor which differentiates successful from less successful companies in their deployment of IS/IT is management's resolve to evaluate IS/IT investments before and after they occurred. Without a review after the event there is no point in having any sophisticated system of investment evaluation and priority setting.

Summary

Creating an appropriate environment to enable the successful deployment of IS/IT requires three aspects of management to be brought together as follows:

1. There should be a means of ensuring that the strategy reflects the business strategy.

2. That the demand for the different applications reflect the real, critical business needs at any time.

3. That the supply of the systems and technology is both appropriate to the particular needs of each, and is co-ordinated effectively across the different systems.

This chapter has attempted to deal with the third issue, namely the strategy for supply management by using a relatively simple matrix concept to enable management to resolve many of the key supply issues. How the supply is managed should be dependent upon the expected contribution to the business of the different types of IS/IT investments. The application portfolio with the generic strategies described, assists in establishing the mix of approaches required and the best approach in any particular situation. The generic strategies are behavioural and imply a cause and effect relationship – a particular strategy will tend to result in predominantly one type of system, for example, a monopoly strategy will result in a focus on factory systems and produce little innovation or strategic IS/IT development.

The resulting framework for managing IS/IT can be appreciated by users, senior management and IS/IT professionals and hence their differing views can be reconciled more easily. Having established the framework, the particular requirements and issues involved in the development and management of the applications and supporting technologies can be resolved as they arise in a rational and consistent way. The following two chapters address these more specific areas, but throughout these will be discussed within the strategic framework which has been established so far.

7

Delivering the goods

Introduction

The development and delivery of information systems is a challenging process: in the past there have been great difficulties with both the process and all that surrounds it. Some organizations have spent many years developing their corporate competence in systems development but others still fail to produce viable systems which are fit for their purpose. There are too many examples of systems which are too expensive, ineffective, or just inappropriate. In addition, the demands made by strategic systems development can be overwhelming. What we have learned about systems development parallels what we already know about the achievement of large and complex projects in other areas of endeavour. In systems development we are faced with the need to specify requirements in an explicit way and to break down complex activities into tasks which we can understand and monitor. We need to develop ways of estimating costs and schedules which will reduce the chance of overspending or overrunning. Above all, we need to be able to manage multidisciplinary teams of people who may never have worked together before and who may have difficulty understanding each other's point of view.

The construction industry provides examples which can help us to organize our ideas about systems development. Most of us have seen a house being built and are aware of what can go wrong – for instance, the buyer who cannot decide where the dining room hatch is to go, or who interferes needlessly with the building work and creates total confusion; the plumber who ruins the work of the plasterer; or the painter who only half finishes the work. In developing information systems we share many of these kinds of difficulty, but the problems are compounded by the abstract nature of the information system product. Like houses, we have to live with information systems and we must be able to maintain them over the years of use.

The house is something which we can easily visualize and quickly sketch on paper. However what exactly is a quick sketch of an information system going to look like? The hardware – whether a personal computer or multimillion pound mainframe – can be visualized easily, but it is not the total system, just a small part of it. The part which has to be developed is the software – the intangible and invisible collation of instructions to the computer which tells it what is to be done. How do these instructions relate to the familiar parts of a house, for instance bricks, slates, timber and internal fittings? A quantity survey of a house is relatively easy to achieve. However, a simple count of the number of 'components' in a computer system is notoriously difficult to estimate – indeed, it is difficult to agree on what the basic components of an information system actually are.

There are technical problems in information systems development, for example problems caused by the fast rate of change of the technology used to develop computer systems. It is not only the user who is bewildered by ever more sophisticated and powerful hardware and software – every year there are new tools and techniques for the technicians which, even if they are seized upon with great enthusiasm, tend to undermine their capability actually to develop systems. If the way of building house walls was changed every year, it is possible to imagine the ensuing chaos.

Other problems relate to the organizational changes that are taking place. Centralized systems development is giving way to devolved authority and capability at the departmental or operating level of many larger organizations. These changes are good news, but nevertheless they present a considerable challenge to all those involved by further undermining the stability of the systems development process.

The approach which is most likely to resolve the basic difficulties is the same that we would adopt for any complex project. Information systems development has similarities with other areas of endeavour such as construction engineering and consumer product development, but the detail and nature of the end product are very different. Some of the consequences of these differences are discussed later.

Basic systems development

It is common to use analogies to describe the information systems development task, and here we have already used the example of house building to explore some of the basic ideas. All analogies have their limits of course, and it should be apparent already that the nature of an information system, as an end product, is radically different to a tangible physical product. This provides a clue as to the inherent difficulties, namely that the systems development process is concerned more with ideas and abstract models than anything we can touch and feel and therefore suffers greatly from our inability to visualize systems in any simple way.

Consider the simple matter of changes. If we decide to alter the plumbing in a house there is much visual evidence that the new pipe work has been done, for example, bright copper around the new joints, paint which has been scraped off the old pipes, and possibly drops of plumber's solder and copper filings on the floor. However, who can tell when the instructions in a program have been changed? A programmer can make sweeping changes to great volumes of program code in a matter of minutes, and there is no evidence in the programs that this has been done, unless the programmer chooses to leave a comment behind within the program source code. The problems of auditing this type of work, where there is not a shred of evidence that changes have been made, can be insuperable.

We try to deal with these problems by using models to represent our ideas about systems, by putting much emphasis upon the documentation which accompanies the technical work, and by breaking down the work into sensible tasks. We must provide an environment where effective communication between team members is possible. Also, when the pressure is on, we must make more time for review and discussion, not less.

Figure 7.1 shows a simple model for the development process where the area of each activity is intended roughly to indicate the effort involved in each of the various activities. As well as the basic tasks it shows the joint involvement in the initiation stage and the post-implementation review which (in the ideal case) will demonstrate that the objectives of the system have been met. It shows technical activity in the upper part of the diagram and user activity in the lower half – during development there will be a great deal to do for the users. The users must also be concerned in some degree with the technical activities, particularly at the start and end of the project.

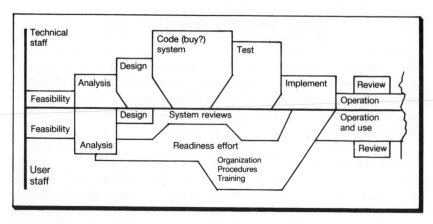

Figure 7.1 Shared development effort

Also, they have their own work to do in preparing for the delivery and handover of the system – there will need to be new organizational arrangements, new office procedures adopted, and staff training to help in adapting to the new system and its accompanying technology. In some cases the users will undertake the whole job themselves by using easy development tools and prototyping methods.

This chapter will first take a traditional view of the basic systems development process, concentrating on the technical activity represented in the upper part of the diagram. Before going further, however, it is worth noting that the critical stages in any project are the areas of joint activity, especially analysis (when the requirement is being investigated), and acceptance testing (when the system is being proved for its suitability and completeness). Any short cuts here will almost certainly guarantee difficulty, delay and additional costs later on, whether during the development process or after the system has been in use for some time. Later in this chapter special attention is paid to the analysis stage, where the users' involvement and understanding of the development process is very important.

Most important, perhaps, is the management of the development process. It is evident in practice that successful projects are often managed directly by the users. Even where the user management has little competence in information systems, the very act of assuming responsibility for a project (and then demanding clear explanations from the technical staff of what they are doing) can make all the difference between success and failure as the business sees it.

Getting started

Figure 7.1 provides a model for the technical and user activities in a project. The detail that lies behind this model will be dealt with later. In the meantime, a good starting point is to consider the different roles which must be enacted. Each person involved with systems development must understand their role, and recognize that each person's perspective on the development process and what it produces will be different. We should not expect that each person understands the others' viewpoints in a detailed way, but just that they should recognize that there are legitimate differences and that they should all respect the common ground – namely, the benefits that the business expects, the timescales involved and the detail of the implementation plan.

The house building analogy is useful again here. In building a house most of us would agree that there are at least four key roles to be fulfilled, as follows:

1. The house buyer who wants the benefit of being able to live in the new house (the user).

2. The architect who has the skill to help the purchaser articulate detailed needs and approve the plans (the business/systems analyst).

3. The craftsman who has the physical skills to put the house together from raw materials, according to the construction plans (the specialist systems developer).

4. The site foreman who has the patience and persistence to see the whole thing through (the project manager).

It is of course possible to adopt a number of these roles at once. The architect might be the purchaser, the purchaser might choose to be both the architect and to oversee the onsite work, or the craftsman might be left to undertake the outline design without the help of a professional architect. This is the same with information systems. There are other supporting roles, of course. There is the builder's merchant who supplies the materials, the building inspector who checks the work against the regulations and the banker who lends the money. Similar roles exist in systems development: the software and hardware suppliers, the budget holder, and so on. As indicated on the above list, the four key roles are the user (purchaser), the

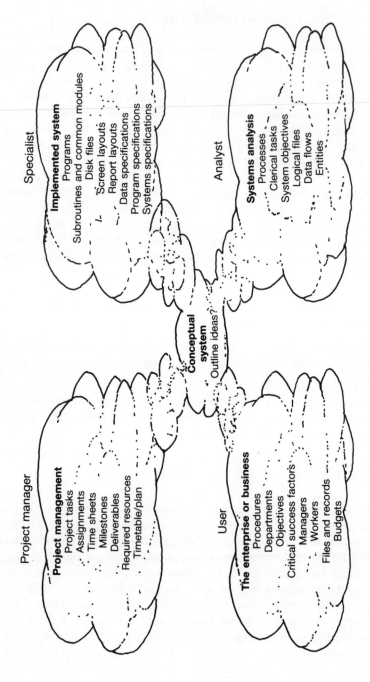

Figure 7.2 Different views of information systems

analyst (architect), the specialist systems developer (craftsman) and the project manager (site foreman). These roles are discussed below and Figure 7.2 shows how the viewpoints of these four parties vary, each seeing the system through different eyes and with a radically different frame of reference.

User (the purchaser)
Users are those who want to have the benefit of the use of the completed system. They must be satisfied at the earliest possible stage that the system will provide the expected benefits, and they must see evidence of progress from time to time while the system is being developed. The extent to which they are involved in the central stages of development varies.

The world of the end user is one of departments and employees, of business objectives and critical success factors. The user will have a good understanding of the business but it may be instinctive. The various business functions, processes, activities and tasks may be so obvious to the user that he or she never thinks to explain them to the system developers. The user will see the facilities of the system as business transactions, access to information, reports and analyses, and other primary documents such as invoices and statements of account. The benefits are as already discussed, namely that there may be cost savings, efficiency improvements, improved services or completely new business opportunities.

Business/systems analyst (the architect)
The systems analyst is often referred to nowadays as a business analyst, whose overall responsibility it is to describe and document the business requirement in a way the user can understand and which will provide a basis for technical development work.

The world of the analyst is a subtle and demanding one. An analyst must be both creative and receptive – he or she must listen uncritically while the user explains problems, and then move towards the new system by explaining options and the implications implicit within them. Analysts must have good communications skills and have the patience to record all that is being said, and later to prepare and present systems proposals which are complete, coherent, and comprehensible to all parties (including the systems developers as well as the end users). This means taking the informal vocabulary and notation adopted by the user and rephrasing the ideas more formally (just as the architect has to make a rough sketch and then formalize it using standard diagrammatic forms and symbols). The analyst will then prepare an outline project plan showing approximate costs and timescales.

This is a demanding and complex world, out of which the analyst must draw order and meaning from what is so often chaos. Business analysis at this level is much concerned with modelling techniques – these produce abstract representations of what is required, and a logical rather than a physical view of what might fulfil the need: processes, not programs; logical data structures, not physical databases; entities rather than people and things.

Specialist systems developer (craftsman)

The specialist systems development role has been complicated by the rapid evolution of systems development technology. Where once the same person might reasonably have done all of the work, this is now less likely. The responsibilities of specialist systems developers relate to the skill of understanding the development environment, such as the computer language systems, operating systems, telecommunications features and database software. It is a complex world where no single person can or ever will be able to understand everything about the computer, nor even the development tools which are used. The danger, of course, is that the different technical disciplines fail to speak with, and understand, each other.

The world of technical systems developers is a mysterious one to most of us. They must understand the technology, what its limits are, how powerful it is, what it will and will not do, and what is likely to make it complain. When it does complain they understand what it is saying and (one hopes) what to do about it.

Project manager (foreman)

It is inevitable that the three disparate roles of user, analyst and developer need a fourth to hold the whole act together. In the same way that a good foreman will see that houses are built to a proper standard, and that the craftsman understands at least most of what the architect wanted, the project manager holds together the systems development project without actually doing any of the real work. The project manager must have an instinct for problems, the confidence to take decisions and the presence to keep everyone involved on the job productively at work.

The world of the project manager is one of lists of things to do, of schedules and of resource management. Everyone on the project must have something to do, it must all be meaningful, and it must be executed in the right sequence. Checks and controls must be put in place and exercised, progress reports must be written so that other interested parties know what is going on, and the project manager has to try to speak everybody's language and to translate as well as arbitrate between the other roles. Except for the intangible nature of the ultimate work product, the project manager in systems development is faced with a very similar task to any other project manager.

Shared interests

Keeping the different viewpoints in line with each other is one of the keys to success. The following points illustrate what each must share with their neighbours:

- The business people must share certain elements of the system with the analysts: specifically the expected benefits and the basic facilities to be provided.

- The analysts must share something with the technical specialists: for example, the way in which the business needs map into the physical components of the finished system. Each logical process must lead to input and enquiry screens which the technical people then specify and construct, and each logical data file must be incorporated into the design for the physical database.

- The project manager has to keep an eye on everything, of course. He or she is dependent upon the analysis work for the detail which will allow the project plans to be finalized, but his or her understanding of the business and the technical work is equally important. After all, until the analysis work is done, the project manager has no real framework within which to manage. Once this is in place, however, he or she needs to be very clear with the technical people about the tasks which they are asked to do, hence the importance of the work breakdown structure.

- In dealing with the business people the project manager will often have great difficulty in maintaining their level of commitment, and only by fully incorporating the user and their tasks into the project plan will the project manager be able to monitor this. Too many projects move slowly but resolutely to the point where the user cries 'enough, I'm just trying to run a business – just tell me when it's all finished'.

Within each area of specialization there is a great deal of detail of

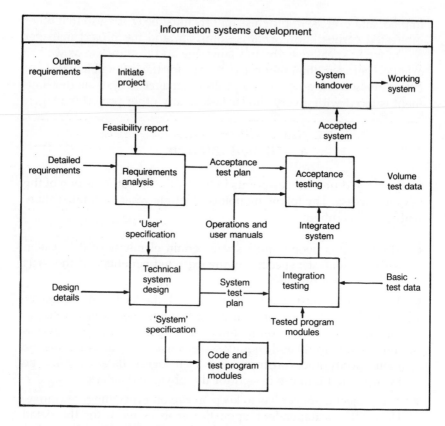

Figure 7.3 The V-model for systems development

concern to only the specialists. Across the boundaries, where there is shared substance to the project, mutual understanding becomes critical to the success and integrity of the work being done and the system being produced.

Once installed, the new systems, and the technology which supports them, can still take up a lot of management time. The overall capacity of the hardware needs to be maintained; systems support and enhancement have to be provided; and internal technology standards and quality control in systems development have to be monitored. Much of this may fall to a technical support group, or there may be a computer operations group which deals with much of this. When the systems are in use there will be queries from the users, and possibly bugs and problems to be fixed.

We have looked at the key areas of systems development, namely the business itself, the business modelling and systems analysis work, the technical development work and project management. We have explored the way different people view the developing system, but what are the jobs they have to do? The next section looks into this.

The main development stages

In the general case the stages of systems development are as indicated in Figure 7.3 – the V-model for the essential work to be done. Each stage includes detailed work which produces 'deliverables', the material evidence that work has been done and which represents the only reasonable basis for agreement, approvals, quality assurance and a baseline for further work in the succeeding stages.

Consider, for example, the required content of the three main deliverables shown at the left-hand side of the V-model, which make up the vehicle for getting the project started and then progressing it through the first stages. The feasibility report provides a broad overview of the departments and jobs which will be affected, the business function which will connect with (or be subsumed into) the new system, and some guidelines based upon the overall information systems strategy to help the project team. Also, it will include commercial and financial analyses demonstrating the technical, operational and economic feasibility of the proposal, and it will document the expected benefits. The user specification provides the detail which clarifies at all levels who will be affected, the specific business tasks which will involve the new system, and the data structures to be employed within and without the new system. The detail within the system can be left in outline – what is most important here is to define the man–machine boundary so that the connections with the real business world can be clearly stated. The system specification concerns technical details rather than the real world of the business and the user. It must deal with the way in which the system is to be implemented, the computer hardware resources required, the structure of the programs and subroutines inside the computer, and the way in which data will be stored on the storage devices in computer files.

Each case seems different, but in fact there is in each one a need to represent resources (people or things) which will support the system in use, processes (business function, tasks or computer programs) which will be executed by the resource, and data which will be processed by the system. This generic division between resource, process and data is important and runs through the various models of systems at all levels. The problem, then, is to find ways in which we can represent resource, process and data structures and the way in which they relate to each other. This is considered in more detail later in this chapter.

On the right-hand side of the V-model we see the emerging system being put through different stages of testing and ultimately being handed over. The detail of module testing, integration testing and acceptance testing is beyond the scope of this book, but acceptance testing is importance because it is the stage at which the user begins to take responsibility for the finished system and it is the last real opportunity to raise queries and change requests.

Any non-trivial development project will require a staged approach in order to give management a proper degree of control, and to give technical staff the chance to work on large complex systems in a modular way. The V-model gives a framework within which we can establish the required stages. It shows clearly the close relationship between the early and late stages (analysis and acceptance testing) and the central stages (design and systems testing). The graphic device of proceeding from the top left-hand corner down to the lower centre and then up to the top right-hand corner reinforces the idea that development takes place at different levels. It is the test plans which establish the horizontal connections in practice, there being different kinds of testing needed. The differences are very important. The V-model is the most useful starting point for a general discussion of systems development at a broad level. It can be used to define the most important deliverables, and it can be manipulated at a more detailed level to show the different approaches to prototyping and other variations on the basic theme.

The main activities

In a software house or in the information services department of a large organization it is typical to find that there is a well specified process for systems development. The stages will be detailed down to task level, the form of the deliverables that are to be produced will be very clearly stated, and perhaps there will be a policy statement on what level of authority is needed for signing off each stage of the work. It would be a mistake to presume that there is just one correct view of all systems development. Nowadays a more fluid approach is taken to the overall task which allows more freedom in allocating responsibility, work assignments and deliverables. A more general view is that the users must establish their purpose, express their needs, and then commission the development of the system, whether by procurement of a package or by bespoke systems development services. We will now consider the main activities shown in Figure 7.3.

Project initiation
A project should not be started until there has been sufficient discussion about its purpose, timescales, the approach to be adopted and the authority required to see it through from start to finish.

Out of the initiation stage should come a simple feasibility report which states clearly the expected benefits, the cost and scheduling limitations, and how the project is to be resourced. There may be connections with, and dependencies upon, other projects working in related areas, and the user's involvement needs to be planned. The way in which a project is bounded (in terms of the part of the enterprise which is affected and the people to be involved) is important to its success. Further decisions will deal with any need to go outside for ready-written software packages or for contract workers to provide special skills. These are the sort of decisions to be made before real work starts.

Requirements analysis
Requirements analysis concerns getting the user to identify needs, problems and expected benefits. The main deliverables are a statement of the functional requirement (sometimes referred to as the user specification or the requirements specification), and at least the outline of an acceptance test plan which will stand as the main reference point during the later stage of acceptance testing.

Historically, this process has been ill defined, and fraught with difficulty and misunderstanding. Nowadays, it is subjected to the discipline of structured methods and is becoming better understood. It is very important to the success of the project, and must be seen as the area of greatest investment of time and effort. The methods and techniques used for requirements analysis are discussed in more detail later in this chapter.

Systems design
Systems design concerns matching the requirement to different technical solutions. Typically it leads into programming, but at this

119

stage it is sometimes necessary to consider any ready-written packages which may provide a quick solution, to look at interfaces with other existing systems, and possibly to consider the reuse of existing system components.

As well as producing a detailed technical specification for programming work (or the technical content of an invitation to tender in the case of package procurement), this activity should produce a systems test plan which will stand as the main reference point during systems testing. It is possible usually to finalize the documentation to be used in regular operation of the system – both by the users themselves (the user manual), and in the case of larger systems the operations staff who run the computer room (the operations manual).

The design stage creates the bridge between the user's need and the hardware and software capability. It is concerned with mapping the business need (as recorded by the analysis work) into a technical solution, and with the addition of the physical design details which ensure that the system is reliable, secure and of adequate capacity.

Module coding and testing (programming)
It may be more appropriate to call this construction – the word coding refers to the practice of writing down program code in a programming language (such as Cobol, PL/1 or Basic). These languages are indeed made up of codes which can be written in a way to make the computer do its job. The newer languages for systems development (often referred to as 'fourth generation languages' or '4GLs') are less concerned with coding and more concerned with higher level language statements which are much more powerful and more akin to natural language. It is comparable to building a house more quickly than is possible with conventional bricklaying and carpentry techniques by using prefabricated components. However, the new way is fraught with potential difficulties while it is still novel.

The time taken in this stage of development is now diminishing. Most of the intellectually demanding work will have been done, and the work of the programmer becomes less demanding as systems development techniques advance. (We will not be very much concerned with programming itself here.) Out of this stage come program modules tested by the programmer which (having been tested individually) have to be brought together and tested together as a part of integration testing.

Software integration testing
Software integration testing concerns the technical correctness and

cohesion of the system. For example, it is necessary to ensure that the system complies with the technical specification, that it performs correctly and with adequate speed, and that it will not collapse under the anticipated operating conditions.

The integration test should be the subject of a plan which ensures that all the particular decisions and assumptions from the design stage are satisfactory, and that the basic 'function, fit and form' of the systems modules are as required, for instance do all the modules co-operate with each other?; can we be sure that the system will not print out a bill for £0.00p?; what happens when the disk storage space runs out?; what happens if the computer operator forgets to mount a magnetic tape file?; etc.

Acceptance testing
The final stage is to satisfy the users that the system is ready for their use, and that it reflects all of the requirements that were originally specified. Acceptance testing is perhaps the least understood stage of development. It may be a long time since the original requirement was specified and the business might have moved on. There may have been many changes during the elapsed time of the project, all of which work against cohesion and completeness in the finished product. Acceptance testing must include a considerable investment of the user's time to ensure that all is well. For example, is the system easy to use?; can achievement of all the expected benefits be anticipated given the actual function and capability in the new system?; is the look and feel of the system right, and are the screen layouts and transaction dialogues appropriate for those who will have to work with the new system?; etc.

This overview of the main stages masks the detailed task assignments that typically will be required. In developing a project plan it will be necessary to go to at least one further level of detail, and possibly two.

Responsibilities

Figure 7.4 shows how the tasks of development may be assigned to the people involved. The detail may vary (we shall return to this in the next chapter), but the shift in responsibility shown is important, illustrating how the user is involved at the start and the end, and the different technical skills in between.

Development task	End-user management	End-user staff	Analyst	System designer	Programmer	Project manager
Initiate project	R	I	?			?
Analyze requirement	I	I	R	I		?
Design system	?	I	I	R	I	I
Construct system				?	R	I
Integrate and test			I	R	I	I
Acceptance test	I	I	R	I	I	I
Handover and use	R	I	I			?

Key:

R   Responsible
I   Involved
?   May be involved

Figure 7.4   Shifting responsibility in systems development

Is requirements analysis the key to success?

In the early days of systems development, requirements analysis was a 'black art'. It was so poorly understood that it was barely visible in the average project plan. However, nowadays it receives more attention than any other stage in systems development, and the methods and techniques employed are very refined.

Previously, the only graphic techniques for modelling systems were based on flowcharting symbols designed for the technician and signifying disk files, magnetic tape files and the now obsolete elements such as paper tape and punched cards. This is equivalent to presenting the house buyer with a detailed view of a house, one room at a time, with so much technical annotation about building materials and instructions that it is impossible for the inexpert eye to make a judgement about what is proposed. However, today we have an armoury of diagrammatic techniques to help. The general approach is to try and devise a business level representation of systems which can be regarded as a model, built to rules which are easy to understand but rigorous. The techniques provide sufficient discipline to optimize our approach to the problem and avoid the obvious traps.

Now consider one of the traps. A strong temptation is to use the organizational or geographic model to label systems, such as the 'warehouse system', the 'personnel system', the 'head office system', or the 'Newcastle system'. However, it is no longer sensible to bound a system using organizational or geographic limits. The systems which provide an enterprise with real commercial advantage are those which are shared across the organization thereby permitting it to operate in a more integrated and timely way. The organizational model of an enterprise is not adequate as a foundation for the conception and definition of information systems and it actually leads to severe difficulties where function and data are to be shared.

A more considered approach to business modelling gives the following quite separate considerations:

- The organizational elements (departments, units, etc).
- The jobs that the people do (business function).
- The information that people work with (files and reports).
- The things of concern about which data are kept (customers, products, branches).

Diagrammatic models can give an accurate representation of these different perspectives on the business.

The key to good requirements analysis is the ability to put aside the more traditional models and to focus on information. Familiar diagramming techniques have been adapted to deal with this need and they have been incorporated into defined methods for development, redressing some of the imbalance towards technical issues. Further, there are now highly developed tools which support these methods and techniques making them more productive and manageable.

Methods, techniques and tools

A method for requirements analysis uses a defined set of activities employing defined techniques which will, by and large, permit a group of people to develop solutions to information systems problems in an orderly, manageable and repeatable manner. Most methods embrace all of the requirements analysis phase and some of the adjacent phases (feasibility and design).

At the time of writing, methods are offered mostly on a proprietary basis packaged with consultancy, technical support and training, but the detail of the different proprietary methods is converging and it is now increasingly within the public domain. The United Kingdom government has forced one particular method – structured systems analysis and design method (SSADM) – into the public domain by requiring its use on all non-trivial central government projects. It is also used widely elsewhere. As confidence in methods increases, and as more people gain the required skills, it must be expected that their use will become familiar to many business people. The tools supporting the new techniques for systems development are evolving quickly and will provide repositories for data about information systems. In due course they will permit a more rapid development of the business information systems that are needed.

However, we must not rush ahead. Instead we must look briefly at the primary techniques and examples of the models (usually diagrammatic) which they produce. The techniques are often seen as falling into two kinds, namely process (or function) analysis and data analysis. Both techniques can be learned easily by business people as well as technical specialists.

Process (or function) analysis

The functionality of a business application can be very complex, but in fact it is this analysis of business processes which often provides a most fruitful starting point. Users tend to be action oriented and warm more quickly to a discussion about what they do rather than the abstract structure of the information they are dealing with. There are two kinds of diagram frequently associated with function analysis, namely the decomposition diagram, or tree structure, and the data flow diagram which is a network representation of the dynamics of data moving through the business.

Decomposition diagrams
The decomposition diagram deals with problems of complexity in business function by dividing the problem into parts one level at a time. A familiar example of a tree diagram is the organization chart which shows how a company is divided into divisions, which are subdivided into departments, which are then further divided into groups, and so on down to individuals. Another familiar example is a bill of materials, which shows how a complex product is divided into assemblies, subassemblies and components.

In information systems requirements analysis, decomposition diagrams are used frequently to show the structure of the processes within a system, both at the higher levels (overall business function)

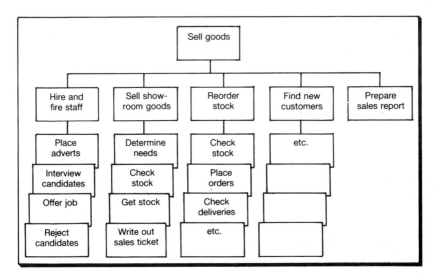

Figure 7.5 Function decomposition

and at the lower levels (structure of individual processes such as computer programs). Figure 7.5 provides a simple example based upon a retail showroom which recruits its own staff and is involved in some direct sales as well as cold calling.

The decomposition diagram is a powerful device useful in the earliest stages of specifying a system to tabulate in a structured way all that goes on. It provides the basis for the initial scoping of a project at a detailed level.

Data flow diagram
Data flow diagrams show how data (and sometimes goods) flow from one point in a business (a point of storage or distribution, say) to another (such as sales). The rules for developing data flow diagrams are relatively simple and all users should be able to understand them if they are constructed properly and presented carefully. Users can check the diagrams for completeness and accuracy far more easily than the pages and pages of text which are the only real alternative. Users will often choose to get involved with the development of the diagrams although this cannot be done without proper training.

Figure 7.6 shows the four notations used to represent the basic elements of a data flow diagram in the SSADM method, namely process, data flow, data store and external entity (or outsider). The

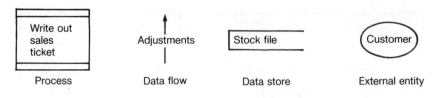

Figure 7.6 The elements of a data flow diagram

best way to become familiar with these diagrams is to use them extensively. Consider the further detail of the retail showroom depicted in Figure 7.7, and note that as one data flow diagram it provides additional details about just one of the legs in the tree structure of Figure 7.5. Note also that it shows the flow of goods as well as data.

Data flow diagrams are developed using rules which govern how they are drawn, how they relate to one another, and how they relate to the more detailed specification material which supports them. While management will not be involved routinely in actually creating them, it behoves everyone in a business to learn how to read them and how to make judgements about their quality, cohesion and completeness.

The diagrams given here are merely illustrative of the way function decomposition and data flow diagrams are used, but in a real case a function decomposition would be more likely to show between fifty processing elements (in a small system) through to several hundred

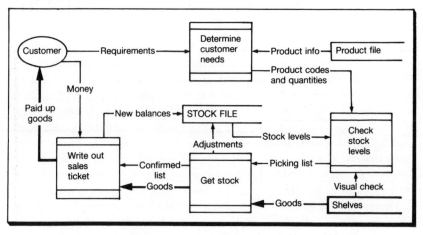

Figure 7.7 The data flow diagram

(in a large system). There might be twenty data flow diagrams in a medium-sized system showing details of about one hundred and fifty processing elements, and the data which flow within and among them. The total number of detailed elements (processes, flows, stores and outsiders) in these twenty data flow diagrams could be as many as one thousand.

Data analysis

The other kind of analysis is concerned with data, and almost completely ignores the functionality of the system. Data analysis is a demanding discipline which is founded in mathematical theory ('relational algebra') and it is beyond the scope of this book to deal with it in any detail, however Figure 7.8 provides a very simple example of its essential product which is the entity model (or logical data structure diagram). These diagrams are deceptively simple. Their development out of data analysis can be an arduous business based upon minute inspection of dozens of business documents and protracted negotiation about the meaning and significance of the data contained therein. Equally (and somewhat paradoxically), these entity diagrams can be produced very rapidly by a brainstorming process. In just a few minutes a good analyst can get a firm grip on the most unusual businesses by using these diagrams as a brainstorming tool.

The entity model tells us nothing about the dynamics of a system but a lot about the static relationships between its fundamental information components. The essential definition of an entity is 'any thing about which we may wish to keep information'. In the entity

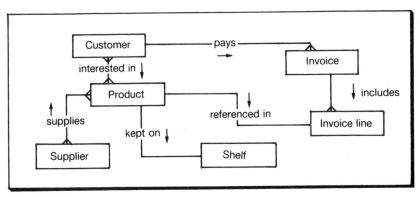

Figure 7.8 The entity model

model all these things are equal, but they may represent people (customer, employee), organizations (operating company, regulatory body), product (stock item, non-stock item), locations (shelf, head office), moments in time (approval, sale), or even completely abstract notions (project, idea). This ability to render such disparate things equal in information terms is the main strength of the entity model. Note how one can 'read' the entity model (see Figure 7.8), for example 'customer interested in product', or 'customer pays invoice'. One other important property of these entity models is that they are very likely to be the only model which can embrace on a single page the totality of an enterprise or business unit. This makes them even more important.

Variations on a theme

Although there has been a history of difficulty with the development of information systems, the basic processes which must be undertaken are now well understood and are being widely adopted. The following kinds of argument have become quite familiar:

- The development of complex systems needs the sort of discipline that is inherent in the world of engineering.

- A system needs to be thought of as an assembly of parts, each of which is properly constructed to fit in with the others, rather than as a homogeneous whole.

- The process of systems development is more manageable when it follows the traditional engineering project cycle of requirements analysis, technical design, construction and testing.

Systems development not incorporating these kinds of ideas is impossible to estimate accurately and can result in systems of poor quality, which perform inefficiently and which are difficult to maintain.

Today new moves are evident which are intended to ease potential problems further – by providing looser frameworks for information systems development and by allowing a more flexible approach – but still based upon firm ground rules. There is something of a competition between the engineering school and the informal approach (often referred to as prototyping).

Systems development in the strategic context

Systems development has been seen for at least twenty years in a rather singular way. For many years the differences between different kinds of project seemed to be of no great concern and one can quote examples where projects which were experimental in nature were given the full treatment – armies of technical designers and programmers working to very rigorous standards – and on the other hand there were critically important projects that were implemented on a 'wing and a prayer'. In the face of any difficulty, the inclination would be to introduce more particular standards, more rules and more procedures, in order to tighten up the way that systems were being produced. This is appropriate in some cases but not in all. The analysis of current and future potential of systems using the strategic grid (see Figure 6.1) gives a framework which is very enlightening and extremely effective in planning the detail of development projects. We will now review it and interpret systems development in each quadrant in turn, expanding upon some of the introductory comments made in the early part of Chapter 6.

High potential
A small proportion of high potential applications will ultimately provide strategic opportunities and help to secure the future of the company. An organization which refuses to accept the need for high potential activity will have great difficulty making progress in the face of competitive and economic forces, whereas one which nurtures and sustains experimental attitudes will never be short of sound, well qualified and potentially useful ideas.

How does one go about systems development in this quadrant? Not with meticulous attention to standards, nor even with large teams of technicians drafted in to make up the numbers. Development in this part of the strategic grid has to be done by (or in very close conjunction with) the user whose idea it is. The objective is not to change the world, but to qualify an idea as a good one. Once this qualification is achieved, when everyone agrees that the idea is important and when the rest of the company has agreed to take it on board, then the style of development will have to change. However, until it is qualified development needs to be fluid, exploratory, and as rapid as possible. There is no benefit in protracted development – every effort should be directed towards the qualification of the idea and as quickly as possible. If the idea proves to be a good one then it can be progressed, but if it is not then it can be discarded. Survival in high potential systems development activity is just as much about learning to live with failure as well as enjoying success.

Strategic

The strategic systems development project needs to have the total support and commitment of the user management and staff. The development of the requirements analysis must be done with the business in mind, and with more attention to what might be done than what is done now. Thus business analysts are required, not technical analysts. A good business analyst is difficult to find and a technical systems analyst given responsibility for the conception and specification of a strategic system will create difficulties all round. A technical systems analyst must be trained in business skills in order to make a useful contribution in the development of strategic systems. Further, the tools that are used by the analyst must be appropriate. It will be necessary to formulate and model ideas about the new system from fairly flimsy ideas seeded in corporate objectives, critical success factors, and the other stuff of strategic analysis. It is important, therefore, that the analysts are able to create good business models which will help all those involved to assure themselves that the proposals are complete and appropriate.

The construction stage in the strategic development project cannot afford to get bogged down in detailed work, but equally it cannot be short circuited. The system must work and to some extent it will have to integrate with existing systems, but not at a very detailed and complex level. It is important that strategic systems are built quickly and competently. Efficiency in their operation is not as important as effectiveness, but nevertheless, the development team must try to forecast the workload levels and ensure that there is enough computer power to sustain the system, even if later it will be re-engineered to make it more efficient.

Testing of the system is important also. There must be carefully prepared test plans which will allow the user to test the function and facility of the system, and to demonstrate its quality and capability against the original requirements specification. Finally, at handover, it will probably be quite impractical to undertake 'parallel running' because of the changes which the system brings. As in the case of the 'Big Bang' in the City of London (an extreme example of a strategic system), one day the old system is used and the next day the new one is used. Trying to live with two systems running concurrently is meaningless when they do not necessarily function in the same way.

Factory
There are fewer mysteries to the factory system. The application is likely to be well known, it is probably common to all the main players in a certain industry, and there may well be packages available which provide a suitable vehicle for implementation (although they are not always cheap – six-figure prices are common for the larger mainframe packages). The larger, more forward thinking companies often find themselves putting these systems together first, the hard way. In fact they may be seen the first time around as strategic because only the larger companies can afford the very high development costs and they justify the expense on the basis of consolidating their dominance of the market. When the ideas have matured the systems then become available from software suppliers (sometimes in the form of a modification of the original system developed by a main player), or if preferred they can be developed in-house more cheaply because the application has become better known and there will be people around who can be hired for their experience and knowledge of the application.

Thus, development projects which are dealing with factory applications systems may find packages to be more suitable than bespoke development. The system still needs to be specified, however, because a good package will provide many options and there will be work to do in setting it up properly. Although a package is the primary vehicle for implementation, it still has to be evolved into the end-users' application system. It is a mistake to confuse the two. If a user decides that problems will be solved by putting in someone else's application system, then this will be a self-deluding step. Even a package will lead to some programming work because other factory applications systems will have to co-exist with the new one and will need to be adapted to interface with it. As some of us already know, adapting an existing system can be much more difficult than building a new one from scratch.

The analysis of a factory system can be done by specialists rather than by generalists, i.e. the technical specialist is probably more appropriate here than the business analyst. The technical skills become very important because efficiency and resilience in a factory system are important. Depending upon the hardware and software environment, skilled database and teleprocessing specialists will be needed, and also systems programmers who can tune the mainframe to give the last percentage point in efficiency. At the testing and handover stage, parallel running will probably be a better approach because we are trying to maintain rather than change the status quo.

Support systems

Support systems are in some senses the most difficult to generalize. They are systems which have little or no current or future strategic relevance, and the temptation is to invest a minimum and to go wherever possible for absolutely standard packages even if they do not fit well – the presumption being that we can change the way we do things to fit the package. Consider an application dealing with Statutory Sick Pay (SSP) record keeping requirements in the United Kingdom, for example. It is unlikely that anyone, other than a software house selling personnel management packages, is going to see this as strategically important – the personnel department of a typical company can almost certainly be persuaded to fit its procedures around a standard SSP package, although the personnel staff may really believe that they ought to have a special system of their own. There are some cautionary points to be noted, however.

For example, a support system needs a degree of requirements analysis to be certain that it is truly a support system. Interfaces with other systems must be investigated because any strong links to factory or strategic systems might affect our view of things – perhaps the support system is not a support system at all? The users' commitment must be assessed to ensure that they really require the system and that they are willing to manage the development project and deal with procurement of packages and the ultimate cut-over to the new system. Support systems do not justify the use of scarce, skilled systems development resources which are deployed more usefully in the other three strategic quadrants.

Having said this, we might remember an example such as American Hospital Supplies, which started with a single customer who wanted to go online – a support project, surely, as it was originally conceived, but so obviously strategic when later seen in the competitive context! The classification of applications can change, either because of a change in the business context, or because we simply choose to regard it differently when it makes business sense to do so.

Horses for courses

What we have learned from the above review of the strategic grid is that there cannot be and must not be a singular view of the systems development task. It is essential that there is some flexibility so that the profile of each development project can be specified individually with appropriate tools and technical skills, and the right degree of user involvement. Indeed, at one end of the scale we must provide for users who want to do their own thing, and at the other we must provide for meticulously built core systems which will be efficient, reliable and economic to maintain. Regrettably there is little evidence that the typical information systems department sees it this way, although there are examples of companies which provide facilities for end-user computing and 'multiple choice' paths for large scale systems development. This provides some basis upon which to incorporate the ideas of the strategic grid.

The effect of providing choice is to promote the importance of project management. Whether it is the end user or a large team of people, the opportunity to get it wrong can outweigh the benefits of providing flexibility. It is essential to classify and plan projects within the overall applications portfolio in a way that is appropriate to the business needs and the available resources. It is possible to channel and take advantage of the user's enthusiasm and to optimize the deployment of scarce central technical resources. However, by providing options the risk is increased of the wrong development path being chosen.

From the basic V-model for systems development (see Figure 7.3) we could either develop a much more detailed approach to development – the rigorous engineering approach – or we could relax it somewhat. We might replace one of the seven basic stages with an alternative procedure which gives flexibility where needed. We might wish to acquire a package or we might just wish to work to a simpler model.

Prototyping

Prototyping is becoming more useful to the world of business information systems as the methods and tools that make it possible become better understood. In order to understand what is involved consider a prototype motor car, which is built as an approximation to the intended final product but not in the same way as a production car. It incorporates enough of the design ideas for the final product so that the design can be validated and the car rendered manufacturable. Essentially, a prototype is functional and it works, but it is not intended for sale and use by regular customers.

The same argument can be adopted in developing information systems (see Figure 7.9). A prototype can be developed which is 'quick and dirty' and which helps to clarify the detail of the requirement when it is uncertain what is required at a detailed level (for

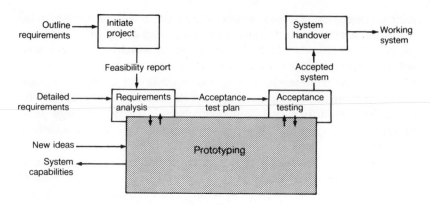

Figure 7.9 One view of prototyping

example in strategic applications). Having developed the prototype, it will probably be thrown away and the proper system built in the conventional way. However, we may choose to keep the prototype and use it, though this is high risk, but this may suit our needs when we are exploring the potential benefits of high potential systems. Prototyping is an approach that will suit end-user computing where the development task is localized, informal and low risk.

In choosing to prototype we are discarding the basis for control – the phases of our project – and reducing the clarity with which we can measure and assess progress. We have to be certain, therefore, that the scope of the project is clear and that there are some alternative controls in place. The primary mechanism for control would normally be the review process where the prototype is assessed for features and capabilities, and compared with the results of a previous review – while we can perceive change we can argue that progress is being made. Alternatively, we can take the cruder approach of applying cash or time limits to force a conclusion to a prototyping project.

The engineering approach

The opposite to prototyping is to put in much more detail in the project plan, apply more control, and invest more heavily in project management. This might be termed the engineering approach because it uses the same meticulous approach which engineers adopt in the large complex projects in other areas, such as large construction and electrical engineering projects. The effect on the V-model diagram is to add a great deal of detail. This is not appropriate for medium and small sized companies where the costs cannot be tolerated because it is easy to double or treble the cost of a project undertaken in this way. It might suit the purposes of a software house, a bank or an airline, however. In the software house, the engineering approach is the only way in which a high level of quality and maintainability can be assured and the costs in this case can be offset against lower support and maintenance costs in the longer term. Should it fail, an airline system might affect the safety of people and a banking system might jeopardize the security of money which is invested. Therefore, for these sorts of reason the expensive engineering approach will be justifiable. It is likely that in future safety critical systems will have to be developed to very exacting standards.

Buying a package

Another more common situation is the purchase of a package – either ready to run or as a bespoke system (see Figure 7.10). When someone else does the detailed design and programming work we can avoid getting involved in this expensive activity, and a package will be fully tested on handover if it is from a reputable source. By eliminating the

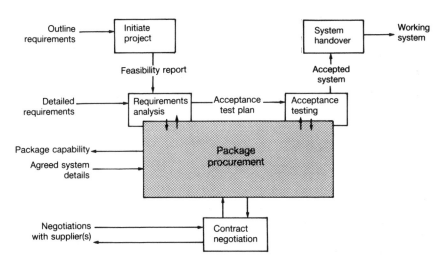

Figure 7.10 Buying a package

135

detail of design and programming the effect on the basic V-model diagram is visually the same as prototyping, but in substance it is very different. A degree of requirements analysis will still be needed although too much analysis will work against our interests, because there is less likelihood that a suitable package will be found. It is better that a well known package is chosen which is based upon good business practice, to which the business can be adapted. Very often a business can be improved in this way. Computerizing a business mess will merely produce a computerized mess – better to buy a package that helps to tidy up.

Third parties are introduced as soon as a package is considered, so there are other jobs to be done. Contracts must be drafted and approved, quality controls put in place and (when buying a bespoke system) progress reporting procedures implemented which will ensure all parties communicate effectively.

End-user computing

End-user computing is a special consideration which can undermine the effectiveness of information systems if not properly managed. There are two kinds of end-user computing – firstly entirely local systems which are implemented with spreadsheet and other general purpose software tools, and secondly decision support systems which rely on access to data from operational systems.

In the first case it helps to provide standard packages with which the users can work. This ensures that a proper level of help and support can be provided and it can economize the cost by volume purchase agreements. In the second case there are wider issues of access control, data integrity and ownership, information centre organization and management, and the need to provide basic definitions of the meaning of different data types.

The role of the information centre dedicated to the support of end users is a developing one. The idea that we can economize by providing specialist support is an attractive one. If users can be supported in an appropriate degree of self help activity the specialists can be deployed more effectively – ratios of 1:70 or more are quoted. By organizing end-user computing with limited central support up to seventy users can be supported adequately by each specialist. Naturally, the skills of these specialists have to be considered – the average programmer will not do. Someone with patience and an ability to talk to the end user in the users' language is needed. At the same time they must have an instinct for the end-user application which is actually the tip of some corporate iceberg (it is essential that substantive systems development is not hidden in the guise of a local support system) and they must be able to solve technical problems originating in complex mixtures of hardware, systems software, applications software and networking equipment.

Summary

Deciding how to reconcile the tools and methods of systems development with the strategic grid is no trivial task, but the general nature of what can be done should now be more clear (see Figure 7.11). Where the users are involved, there is the further complication of ensuring that they understand and are committed to their involvement and that the tools and methods used are appropriate to the non-

	Turnaround	Strategic	Factory	Support
Project definition	Loose and open. Cost limits rather than firm objectives. User led.	Strong, manager-led team. Broad brief. Strategic tools for the job.	Technically led team, tight definition of standards, meticulous project management.	Use external services if possible. Let the user manage the project.
Analysis of requirements	Exploratory and informal. Use prototyping ideas to establish details.	Creative and broad in scope. Carefully document the work. Reviews	Contained but thorough. Attention to interfaces. Work to efficiency	Limit to essential needs and possibly to isolation of the system at hand.
Build system	Rapid and iterative. Use peer reviews to identify weakness and firm ideas	Innovative but carefully planned and rapid. Limited prototyping.	Contract out, or use packages where possible. Aim for efficiency	Avoid undue effort! Contract out and assume packages will do.
Test system	Informal.	Well planned, meticulous and biased to the end user needs.	Exhaustive, with a bias to the technical and the efficiency of the system.	Assume it works? Otherwise minimize effort.
Handover	Crossed fingers, and an expectation to re-work with user experience.	With great care! Big Bang may be the only way. Lots of education.	With great care! Parallel run will probably be the best way.	Minimize effort and ensure user self-sufficiency.

Figure 7.11 Systems development and the strategic grid

specialist. However, when everything comes together properly the results can be spectacular. It is a challenge for both business and information systems management to achieve the right balance of innovation and rigour in every project, in order to maximize the chances of success.

The important message is that it is not appropriate to treat all development projects in the same way. The incorporation of prototyping ideas will help in the upper part of the strategic grid and packages are likely to be more helpful in the lower half of the grid. Where systems are critical, sound information systems engineering methods are needed; where systems are not critical, a more casual approach is in order.

8

Marshalling the IS resource

The nature of the IS resource

Conventionally much attention is paid to the processes of systems development, in particular the requirements specification stage. Systems which have become operational often receive the least management attention but actually cost more than those being developed. The operational system rarely excites technical management but it is a major concern for business management. A very high proportion of the total cost of a system – taken over the whole of its life – can be attributed to the operational stage and this cost accrues to the user: the proportion of the total cost of a single system that derives from the in-service stage can be higher than 70 per cent. In large part this is avoidable. We are still learning how to build information systems that are more robust and more easily maintained, and there is in any case less need to build our own. It is now possible to acquire large and very capable software packages for routine needs (payroll, accounting, stock management and the like). The advantages of buying a package include the fact that someone else will maintain it, at a known cost.

It follows that the 'information systems resource' is much more than what we see in the development stages. In trying to agree what the IS resource is, we might therefore start with the completed systems which are working for our business, and regard all of the work product from the information systems development task (specifications, programs, manuals and even test plans) as an asset that must be managed. We must also consider the tools of systems development and maintenance (program compiler software, analysis work benches, library management systems and the supporting systems software) as part of the IS resource, just in the same way that plant and equipment is the essential resource of a manufacturing company. Many people argue today that we need to take an inventory approach to managing the IS resource, and some (in the United States and elsewhere) even talk of devising a standard part-numbering scheme for systems and software products which would allow information about the inventory to be shared by all interested parties (much as it is now in the retail food trade).

There is another aspect of the IS resource, of course, namely the people who are involved. The technical staff who have the skills to develop and maintain systems are still in short supply and are likely to continue to be so. In easing the problems of resourcing individual projects it is important to consider user staff (who want the system) as part of the resource available and to involve them productively in the work that has to be done. This leads naturally on to the issue of how the various human resources are organized and where they report in the organization. How much resource should be deployed centrally and how much away from the centre? This has been a major issue and a source of conflict for many years. It is partly a matter of control and accountability, partly about the most effective means of supply management and partly about ownership of the resources and the resulting systems. Effective ways of managing these aspects of information systems resource are considered in the second half of this chapter.

Management issues

There are many management issues in keeping the IS resource together and in making sure that we deploy our efforts in an optimum way. Consider some of the following:

- The information system is made up of very large numbers of technical components or elements (program code, hardware and systems software) which can be thought of as an inventory of parts which needs managing just like any other inventory.
- The system performs business functions – these need to be kept relevant.
- There is documentation which describes these components and

which stands as the entry point when we wish to do anything with them – it must be maintained with the components and must always be updated meticulously.

- The information systems workforce is getting older and there is a shortage of young recruits – we need to organize and deploy the scarce resources that we do have optimally and set appropriate priorities to new development and maintenance work.

- The security of our inventory is a key issue. Some of the components of information systems (especially the data) are extremely vulnerable to malevolence and to acts of God, and it is essential to be able to recover from disasters of one kind or another.

- The whole question of the cohesion of our inventory is a major problem: which components work with which others?; does that which works on one computer work on another? (probably not); how many versions of a program or specification have we got?

- The capacity of an installed computer (especially large mainframes and networks) to do work is very complex to estimate and manage. This is a special skill which is not easily found.

- How do we manage changes and problems when (either in operation or in development) someone decides that the objectives have changed or that we have actually got it wrong and created a problem that needs solving?

- The maintenance of systems in use is, as already mentioned, a considerable task which typically costs more than half of the IS budget.

Security is one of today's major issues as systems become more global, more dependent on networks, and therefore more accessible to those with mischievous intentions. The ease with which machine-readable data can be copied and transmitted and the complex nature of computer-based information systems both help to make the detection of criminal activity extremely difficult. It almost always comes to light by accident, and many organizations prefer not to deal with computer crime in the courts in case it undermines confidence in their corporate and management skills. Worst of all, it is possible to perpetrate a computer crime without entering any corporate premises – it is all possible over the telephone.

The operation and management of systems which are in use is quite different from managing the development process. An information systems project is much like any other, namely a collection of different people with different skills, assigned temporarily to a shared task. An IT operations department is better organized along functional lines so as to concentrate on the ongoing nature of the task. The modern business depends so completely upon its information technology that much of the management of operational information systems is done from one moment to the next as minor operational crises come and go. The longer-term operational concerns such as security and the need to be able to recover from major disasters are often pushed to the background thereby putting the whole organization needlessly at risk.

Much of the IS resource management challenge can be seen as similar to the challenge to other corporate management who have resource to be managed. Consider manufacturing management. The same attitudes and skills that are successful in managing a stores area containing valuable components will probably help us to deal with the IS inventory with equal success. But the nature of the product we are concerned with means that the following apply.

- It is not material, it is abstract and there is no common basis upon which different parties can easily share their views of what a system is.

- It is possible to change software very quickly indeed and to leave absolutely no evidence that the changes have been made.

- It is very complex, the most simple systems being based upon thousands of elemental components and large systems being based upon millions.

- The context within which we conceive and build systems can change rapidly.

In order to get an understanding of the very great potential difficulties that arise from the nature of the product, this chapter proceeds with a review of six key activities that must be present if the development and use of information systems is to succeed. They are as follows:

1. Documentation management.

2. Software inventory management.

3. Security management.

4. Project management.

142

5. Quality management.
6. Capacity management.

Support for the IS resource

Documentation management

Although software may exist in a material sense on a disk or some other storage medium, this is a machine-readable representation which is of no use to a human who might wish to know the nature, purpose or function of the software. Whereas in a moment we can identify the nature and purpose of a car (and distinguish it from a lorry or a bus), it is impossible to do this when looking at a disk that contains a software system that may or may not be of interest to us. It falls to the paperwork to tell us what a system does for us and how it does it. No doubt many people have suffered the frustration of having to learn how to use software – perhaps a word-processing package on a personal computer – which was not properly documented. If we are acquiring software today one of our primary concerns is the quality of the documentation which accompanies the software and the way in which it will help with installing and using it.

However, how often have we stopped to consider the other documentation that must support a software system? Consider for example the problems of people working in the software development team: they have to rely on documentation to provide a single definition of the developing system; to ensure that different modules in the system work properly with each other when they are put together; and to demonstrate the extent of progress being made to project leaders and management. The role of documentation in achieving all of this is critical. It is primarily through the documentation that a system is rendered comprehensible.

We can summarize the purpose of documentation as follows:

● To provide a human-readable representation of a system for those concerned with its development.

● To record the final form of the system as given to the machine.

● To communicate the state of development to other interested parties.

● To place on record the function and capability of a completed system for the benefit of those who might wish later to correct, improve or enhance it.

● To make available the information and instructions needed by the users of the system.

A system which is to have any significant life has to be documented 'for the record' so that it can be improved and extended. Even the personal computer user who is developing a personal spreadsheet needs to have some record of what has been done, if the spreadsheet is of any significant size and if it is not a one off. In the case of large complex systems it is critically important that the system is well documented if it is going to be developed further in the future. In all but the most trivial situations it is necessary to provide standards for documentation which will give basic helpful guidance to all those using a system. The content and scope of use of each kind of document needs to be clearly understood.

Above all it is the needs of the reader which must be kept in mind. It is not uncommon to find that an IS department has technical standards that deal only with development documentation. User documentation must be provided to help those concerned to use the system. Even better, put the documentation on the computer itself, and publish it through the computer and the terminals which people use, so that a computer-based management system can help by the use of automatic indexes, by providing different levels of access and different levels of detail.

Software inventory management

As we come to rely more upon old systems which cannot easily be replaced we find the inventory approach to managing software helps us to control changes and versions, and gives a basis for rendering software product reusable. This is perhaps the single most important objective which the technical people should set themselves: never to do twice that which need only be done once. It is the need to be able to change systems which undermines our ability to succeed in this otherwise admirable objective.

Dealing with changes can be a most difficult task. Changes may be raised by the user (because his or her business has changed), and by the technical staff (because the technology or implementation strategy has changed). It is important that changes are not dealt with on an individual basis when there are many to be dealt with. They must be evaluated in the overall context of the system and its status (using the technical documentation that is to hand), grouped into remedial work packages and then handled as projects in their own right. Without this process of rationalization the work that derives from uncontrolled changes can wreck the quality and cohesion of an otherwise excellent maintenance plan, and rapidly undermine the viability of an installed system in the operational phase.

Security management

Security and privacy form another complex area for information systems management to deal with. The concepts of accessibility, accuracy and ownership are pivotal in trying to get a grip on this difficult area and the risk of criminal action needs to be assessed. This part of the chapter deals with security of access, the general risks that hang over an installation, and the preventive measures which can be put in place.

Accessibility comes in two guises, namely access to the function of a system, and access to the information contained in it. How do we establish the privileges of these two types of access? Having a user identification (ID) and password (it is the combination of these two which usually provides security of access to a system) is the first step, and will almost certainly tell the system in more precise terms which of its particular facilities the user is permitted to invoke. This is at the level of which of the computer programs one can call and run, be it through a menu facility, command structure, or other dialogue mechanism. But what about the data? If two users are both allowed onto the bill of materials system, are they both automatically allowed to browse through all the data? Or are they to be constrained to the data that they have a legitimate right to look at? Separating out access to the function of a system on the one hand and the information within it on the other is an important step that is sometimes not considered at all.

Some software (and hardware) systems do not recognize this distinction, though other software does. The operations managers need to take a careful look at the facilities provided with their computer hardware and operating software – writing security into a system at the applications software level is not going to provide anything like the same degree of control and may not reduce the risk of malicious access at all.

Equally IT managers have to make sure that data are easily

available to those who have a legitimate right to access. It is not that security controls would get in the way – they should occupy no more than a few seconds at the start of a session – but those data are often locked away in files which can only be accessed by applications programs written many years before. Recently there has been good progress in dealing with this problem. Software is now available which allows the technical staff to scan old programs automatically for the structure and location of the data being used, so that automatic enquiry facilities might be added to the original programs more easily. This process is called reverse engineering and is just becoming viable as a routine operation. (The implications for the maintenance workload could be very significant but it is too early to say whether reverse engineering will also solve the systems mainten-ance problem.)

Risks to the routine operation of an installation include the following:

● Irregular physical access to the building (and all associated prem-ises such as cable trunking, communications rooms, and the like).

● Irregular remote access to the computer system using the com-munications system.

● Computing resources (documentation, magnetic media) being left in insecure places.

● Fire, flooding and power failure.

● Delinquent personnel.

● Lack of adequate recovery plans.

Some of these are not unique to computer installations, but the problems of remote access, delinquent personnel and recovery plan-ning are.

Basic precautions

A simple way of dealing with access problems is to make sure that there is a record of access attempts, so that when a hacker begins to try out his or her ID/password combinations it becomes apparent to anyone who cares to inspect the records. It is astonishing to discover what obvious and predictable passwords are sometimes used. For example, Prestel had to appeal to its users to stop using the password '0000'; systems operators who require access to many systems, and thus have a major problem keeping up with all the passwords, tend to use longer passwords, but just as obvious, for example, '0123456789'. A system can require the user to change passwords from time to time, but most users change it to something like 'FRED' momentarily and then revert to the word that they can remember.

One of the simpler actions to deal with the remote access problem is the 'ring-back' idea. A legitimate user would connect with an intelligent computer, which has the job of managing the 'front-end' of the system and to which the user would give his or her identity. The computer would acknowledge, hang up the phone and redial automatically the telephone number that it has stored against that ID.

Delinquent personnel are much more difficult to deal with. A first step is to ensure that everyone knows what they are supposed to do, what they are allowed to do, and to ensure that there are some measures that will secure the organizational boundaries. Beyond that it gets difficult. The 'virus' or 'logic bomb' has become quite well publicized, and a number of large commercial systems have been reported to have done unexpected things (on anniversaries and birthdays) as well as the better known problems with personal computers. The manager is left with the usual options of checking carefully on backgrounds, keeping close to employees to make sure there are no grudges lurking, and attending to routine matters such as returning card-keys which are not needed, and generally generating and reinforcing an organizational culture which presumes meticulous attention to these points of detail.

Recovery

A way of recovering from all the consequent problems needs to be planned before it is needed. There will be a trade off in the cost of any arrangements which are made to duplicate and maintain facilities (which will support essential systems in the event of major disaster) and the probability that there actually will be a disaster – risk analysis is a way to deal with this. Some steps which might provide easier recovery include the following:

- Acquiring alternative premises with a minimum of compatible equipment.

- Sharing such premises with compatible installations that use the same computer.

- Contracting alternative facilities with one of the specialist companies that specialize in disaster centres.

- Documenting the back-up and recovery arrangements.

- Ensuring that all files, applications software systems and operating software are copied periodically and placed in a distant location.

- Practising the arrangements periodically to ensure that the back-up or recovery plan really works.
- Clearly allocating the responsibility for back-up and recovery with a single manager or supervisor.

Any action needs to be balanced against the cost, and might have to reflect overall corporate policy in the matter of risk management.

Project management

Although systems development projects have been described in the previous chapter, the role of project management in sustaining the IS resource must not be underestimated. The proper application of project management will help to avoid problems because it provides a focus for resolving many of the technical issues. However, the ability of project managers to understand the business issues is also an important factor in achieving success and providing systems which will serve the needs of the business for many years.

Formalized project management methods (such as 'PRINCE' – the United Kingdom government standard – which depends heavily upon 'project boards' and other committee-like devices) define a much broader framework for projects than we have been used to, and work with the system on a total life-cycle basis – from conception to operation and phase-out. As the mix of development activity continues to become more complex the discipline which allows many projects to co-exist, at different stages in the overall life of systems and subsystems, will become an important feature of information systems resource management. Project management is bigger than the individual project and some would say that programme management is the discipline which can handle the conflicting demands of many concurrent projects as well as the maintenance and *ad hoc* work that so often predominates.

Quality management

The total quality management (TQM) approach to quality is popular today, and given the evident difficulty with delivering what the user needs when required and at the expected price, the vogue for quality management in information systems is understandable. TQM is unhesitating and unremitting in its commitment to the 'zero defect' policy. Quality is built in at the start, it is argued, not tested in at the end of the development cycle. The purists argue that investment in testing should be withheld in favour of investing in getting it right first time. It seems that the challenge to IS management out of the total quality management culture is to build software that does not need testing.

How can this be reconciled with the status quo? Surely we must, if we are honest with ourselves, admit that there is often a very high level of defects in the software and systems that we deliver today and that testing (at several different levels) is essential if we are to reduce and eventually eliminate faults and bugs. This is particularly so in view of the current concern with safety critical systems. With increasing dependence on systems in business and life at large and with the responsibility of suppliers to ensure that software products are fit for use, the software engineering attitude is both popular and seems to hold benefits. There are formal schemes (such as assessment and registration under ISO 9000 – the international standard for quality management systems), but without the commitment of management and staff there is no hope of significantly improving quality in the first place, and in maintaining it in the longer term. It is not easy to reconcile the 'hearts and minds' approach to quality with the popular view of a person in a white coat, with broad authority to stop production lines, call in faulty products, and redefine technical standards and requirements.

Consider for a moment the strategic grid (see Figure 6.1). Clearly, any quality management attitude which precludes variations to standards and which adopts a policing attitude will conflict with the needs and attitudes of turnaround (high potential) and strategic applications. On the other hand, the need for excellence in the finished factory system needs the rigorous approach. If we view quality management through the strategic grid we might conclude that the top half is about hearts and minds whereas the bottom half is about metrics and excellent engineering.

Capacity management

The need to monitor the use of a large complex computer system and to plan for its enhancement in good time for future needs is a well understood problem. It is similar to conventional capacity management in many respects, namely the identification of workloads and the breaking down of workload into independent components that can be readily analyzed, estimated and projected into some kind of overall demand model. This is no more than the problem of identifying routings and workstation performance on the factory floor.

The problems with information systems capacity management arise for the usual reasons, namely that information systems are ethereal, intangible and notoriously difficult to visualize because of their complexity and sensitivity to the most unexpected things. Traditionally, operating a large mainframe has been extraordinarily difficult because varying operating systems parameters (memory allocations, channel configurations and the other sorts of things that expert systems programmers have to do) can have a dramatic effect upon the computer's performance.

The capacity management function needs to have an eye on the business so that the future demand is understood in business terms (number of customers, sales orders, invoices, and so on). It needs to be able to relate business activity at this level to transaction volumes in the main operational applications systems. Further, it needs to be able to extrapolate this to the housekeeping activity which makes no direct contribution to the operation of systems for the business, but which is essential to ensure the accuracy, resilience and recoverability of those systems. Finally there is the question of charge-back arrangements and the way in which demand can be managed by manipulating charging structures. The operation of today's real-time systems becomes increasingly like a commodity product marketing operation where demand is elastic, the product can be acquired from multiple sources, and the pricing structure in relation to the perceived value of the product becomes critical in keeping the user or customer happy.

The supporting activities which are necessary to sustain a viable and effective information systems function are several and various, and together they can be seen as an infrastructure which will sustain the information systems resource at a level above the individual project or business application. Managing this infrastructure is a complex challenge largely because there is so much new thinking about the application of techniques like quality management and capacity management. Always one is tempted to make comparisons with other engineering disciplines but we must remember the nature of the information systems resource – it is abstract and intangible. This amplifies many of the problems faced in other disciplines and makes special demands upon those who have to manage it. Interestingly, it is the computer which comes to our aid in trying to handle this complexity and we must expect that management of the information systems resource will rely increasingly upon supporting information technology and – one must hope – good systems for the information systems manager.

Organizational strategies for managing IS/IT

As described in Chapter 4, there is a need to manage IS/IT coherently through the phases of establishing direction in order to ensure that IS/IT investments are related directly to business development; planning those investments in order to deliver the greatest overall benefit; and implementing the systems successfully in order to achieve those benefits. Various more detailed aspects of those three phases have been explained in previous chapters. In Chapter 6 generic or high level strategies were described – these provide guidance as to the best way to manage the portfolio of applications in accord with their expected business contribution. To achieve success these must be brought together into organizational structures and policies, defining how things will be managed, by whom and how the various responsibilities are related. These structures and relationships must be capable of carrying through what has been decided and be able to accommodate and interpret all the changing circumstances which will undoubtedly affect the strategy or its implementation.

The organizational approach must consider a number of key issues, including the following:

- The positioning of IT specialist resources within the organizational structure, where the bulk of the supply capability is located and to whom it reports.

- How the required people and skills are to be acquired, developed and deployed. IS/IT skills are in short supply and those people's expectations have to be satisfied as well as the organization's resource needs.

- How the suppliers of technologies and services will be dealt with and the required resources procured.

- How applications and activities are co-ordinated and controlled in a multiproject, multiuser, multiskilled environment which will cross normal organizational boundaries.

- Ensuring the creation of a culture which enables good interpersonal relationships to exist between business people and IS/IT specialists.

- How conflict and contention for resources will be resolved when they arise (as they inevitably will).

There are undoubtedly other issues. One, which has already been referred to, is how the costs of IT are transferred to the business – traditionally called charge-out. Something which is often seen merely as an accounting or administrative issue, can cause major problems if not considered carefully. The main problem is that charge-out is actually a transfer pricing mechanism and is seen by the business managers as the price they have to pay for IT. If that pricing system is inappropriate then managers may make tactical buying decisions which are inconsistent with the strategy. Much has been written elsewhere about this subject, and it is an aspect of IS/IT management for which coherent policies need to be established and understood by all concerned. The policies should, as far as possible, be related to policies for charging-out/pricing other service functions.

Returning to the organizational issues mentioned above, it seems that wherever the main resources are located within the organization, there is a need to overlay the formal organizational relationships with a further IS/IT management structure. An IS/IT management steering group, or similar, is usually the result. Eighty per cent of major organizations in both the public and private sectors have them. If IS/IT resources are located centrally then the steering group has to ensure the resource is being used appropriately in meeting business priorities. If resources are distributed the steering group has to ensure that applications are developed in the most coherent overall pattern, especially when they could be used across the company. In the first case the steering group is directing the IT department, and in the second it is co-ordinating the business IS/IT activities. Since, as is reviewed below, there seems as yet to be no ideal way of organizing and locating the IS/IT resources, some such steering mechanism is probably necessary. How it should work is examined later.

Centralization vs. decentralization

Viewed from an organizational perspective the history of IS/IT in many organizations has been a struggle for control of resources, between centralization and decentralization. Obviously a number of factors will affect the advantages of either approach, including the geography, the management structure and the culture of the organization. In highly centralized organizations there is a natural tendency to centralize major shared resources such as IS/IT, whereas if managers are expected to behave autonomously the reverse is true. The changing nature and economics of the technology enabled more decentralization in the 1980s, although latterly businesses have recognized that synergy and integration by means of IS/IT offer significant additional benefits.

Equally importantly, in the past, the IT specialists tended to produce systems to meet user needs and the need for co-ordinated and efficient means of production tended to suggest that a central supply mechanism was best. More recently, more systems can be purchased in the form of packages, and users can easily develop some systems themselves, given a degree of technical assistance. Therefore, the IT specialists have had to develop a new orientation which is to provide a service enabling users to meet their own requirements. Often this is manifest in the provision of an information centre or an end user support group, which assists users and co-ordinates the procurement and dissemination of technology.

If a central IT group is allowed to dominate, essentially create a monopoly, a number of problems can result including the following:

● Forcing new systems to integrate with existing (often much older) ones and hence limit the use of packages etc., and an insistence on 'building' everything, resulting in very high levels of internal maintenance.

● Insistence on methodologies being followed in all cases, with achievement of the business benefits being secondary to achievement of the process. Users can become very frustrated.

● Decisions will be heavily technically biased, but normally a conservative view of technology will prevail, with little innovation.

However a highly skilled resource should develop, of a size which enables career development of the IT specialists, and the lack of dependence on key individuals will protect the investments.

Where user discretion dominates the decision making (free market) an opposite set of problems may result, including the following:

● Localized, short-term focus on problems, producing incompatible systems, which also results in a high maintenance overhead (which may be hidden).

● Poor quality control of systems and data.

● Low levels of skill due to scattered resources – with little exchange

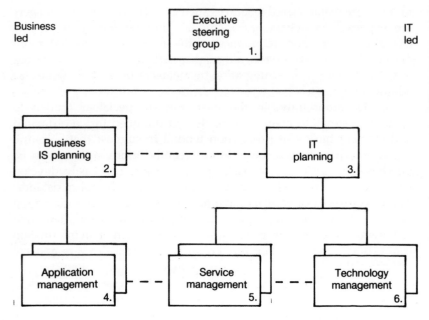

Figure 8.1 Organizational requirements

of skills – resulting in low levels of real productivity in delivering systems.

• Loss of buying leverage with suppliers due to lack of co-ordination of purchases.

On the other hand, the systems will, at least locally, address real current business issues, providing the skills are available to deliver them. Neither of these extremes includes any process of central planning, which is needed if strategic opportunities are to be identified and delivered successfully. Both effectively ignore the role which senior management can and should play in deciding what investments are made. Hence a balance must be found between centralizing and decentralizing, establishing where each is most effective and then adding the senior management role through some executive (or steering group) mechanism. This should not be too difficult to achieve within one business unit or coherent organizational entity, but it is more difficult in a multiunit organization. The rationale explained in Chapter 6 regarding potential cross-unit benefits within the application portfolio offers some guidance, being based on the realities of the business environment rather than the politics of the organization.

Figure 8.1 outlines the major processes which have to be carried out and their interrelationships based on the more detailed arguments presented earlier in this book. The structure not only indicates the major processes which need to be carried out, but also addresses the need to link direction setting, planning and implementation both to get the right things done and to provide feedback and control as discussed in Chapter 4 (see Figure 4.3).

The main responsibilities of each 'box' can be considered as follows, starting at the highest, direction setting level:

1. **Executive steering group**: is a consortium of senior managers including the most senior IT managers, and involves the following:

   (a) interpreting business and corporate strategy and agreeing overall IS/IT policies;

   (b) establishing priorities, resolving contention, agreeing overall expenditure and authorizing major investments;

   (c) setting the overall direction and monitoring business critical projects;

   (d) agreeing the degree of centralization/decentralization, allocating overall responsibility and establishing the right culture and attitudes to achieve co-operation and co-ordination at lower levels.

   Overall they are discharging two major responsibilities as follows:

   (a) the central planning of strategic applications; and

   (b) establishing the appropriate organizational responsibilities and relationships.

   The next level is responsible for converting the overall direction to realizable plans and providing relevant feedback on progress.

2. **Business IS planning**: is an integral part of the business planning process for the unit or major business function, which involves the following:

   (a) co-ordinating and prioritizing all IS activities in the business area, including agreeing budgets, approving proposals and resource allocations to particular projects;

   (b) identifying business needs, opportunities and potential threats and assessing the IS implications;

   (c) ensuring user resources are adequately supplied and appropriate people are assigned to manage the projects;

(d) ensuring the appropriate benefits are identified and achieved, and that business changes associated with systems are managed successfully.

In many cases major projects will cross business boundaries and again this part of the structure is responsible for the co-ordination of activities across those boundaries.

3. **IT planning**: is a line responsibility of the IT senior manager and his or her team and should include the following:

    (a) interpreting external IT trends to the benefit of the organization;

    (b) ensuring resources are deployed to meet the business priorities;

    (c) developing the IT resources and services in line with demand and within the policies agreed. In particular, the development of the skills and approaches to ensure projects can be achieved and productivity is improved over time;

    (d) managing the supply of technology and specialist bought-in services to the organization;

    (e) ensuring that technical risks are commensurate with the business benefits and risks of major investments.

The responsibilities are essentially those of supply side management, namely whether or not they control the activity directly or it has been devolved to the business. To balance this the business IS planning role is to deal primarily with demand side issues. The executive group must resolve or reconcile any demand/supply imbalances.

At the implementation level there are three major processes.

4. **Application management**: is a process which must be led by user management. It is the business which has to live with the real consequences of systems investments and in the long term each part of the business will get what it deserves, depending upon the quality and quantity of the business management applied to the systems' development and operation. This applies both to major systems' developments where the bulk of the resource and skills are provided by the IT department and where the system is resourced totally within the business area. Key aspects are as follows:

    (a) identifying, specifying and quantifying the needs, benefits, resources and costs of any project to enable management to make informed evaluations and establish priorities;

(b) managing projects and installed systems to ensure they meet business needs;
(c) ensuring business changes associated with the systems are understood and implemented, and that user resources on the system are appropriately deployed (especially where projects cross organizational boundaries);
(d) ensuring specialist resources are deployed to meet the contract in the project development, and that ongoing service levels are agreed and met.

5. **Service management**: which may reside wholly within the IT function or be wholly or partly distributed to the business units (especially in large organizations). Such services include systems development, computer operations, information centres, network services, data administration, etc. The service group orientation is towards the applications to ensure the needs are met in the most effective way, and provide the relevant co-ordination and experience transfer across applications, which are inevitably developed over extended periods of time and rarely ideally synchronized. Particularly important are the following:

(a) translating needs into technical and resource implications and developing overall skills and methods accordingly;
(b) monitoring performance to agreed service levels and delivery targets;
(c) ensuring technology is acquired and tested to minimize the risk of application failure;
(d) bringing appropriate (internal or external) specialist resources together to satisfy system requirements;
(e) planning the development of services and associated resources to intercept changing user demand.

The service groups will in some ways act as intermediaries between business people and technical specialists who really have little in common. The people in the service groups must understand both points of view and speak the language of each to ensure effective translation from demand to supply.

6. **Technology management**: unless the organization is a highly diversified conglomerate, managed mainly as a set of investments which are continually traded, if any aspect of IS/IT should remain centralized then it is technology management, namely the management of hardware, core software, telecommunications. All of these require highly skilled specialists to achieve the best from

the technology and to deal with the major suppliers. The key aspects are as follows:

(a) understanding technology developments, formulating options and informing others of the implications;
(b) assessing the capabilities of technologies against known needs;
(c) planning and managing the introduction of new technology (and the migration away from obsolescent technologies) to minimize the risk to existing and future business applications;
(d) supporting the service groups in managing the technology changes associated with changing demand;
(e) ensuring that technical problems can be resolved expeditiously either within the organization or in conjunction with the suppliers.

These lists of responsibilities are not meant to be exhaustive, but to show the range of things that must be managed well over time and to partition those responsibilities in a balanced way between the business and the IT specialists, within a structure which enables effective co-ordination.

Organizational positioning

During the last twenty years the position of the manager whose sole responsibility is IT (hereafter called the IT manager), has gradually risen in the organization. That is not to say the incumbent has always risen with the job, since as the role has been seen to be more important, so the managerial skills required have become greater. The best technician rarely makes the best executive, although until the 1980s most IT managers had a profoundly technical background.

According to all that has been argued before, information and IS applications pervade the whole business and their management is the responsibility of every line manager and their co-ordination a collective executive responsibility, i.e. essentially demand side management. However, there are many aspects of predominantly supply side or IT management which need to be managed together, often centrally. Whether that department should report to the chief executive officer (CEO) or through another executive is a matter of debate and should really depend upon both how critical IT is to long-term business success and how similar service groups within the organization report into the executive structure.

In a bank, for instance, IT is the technology of banking and an IT director would seem logical, not that an IT specialist should necessarily fill the job. In a high technology company where IT is one of a number of technologies, it might well report to a technical director. Where IT is primarily seen as a commercial weapon, critical to the future of the business, such as in retailing, IT is likely to report through a commercial or business development executive. If IT is still only (or seen to be only) an administrative support tool then it may well report through finance (as was often historically the case), or some other essentially administrative/services executive.

Normally as the application portfolio matures and the business dependency increases, so the IT manager migrates up through the hierarchy. At the same time, it is more probable that the person filling the job will come from the business rather than the IT department. In reverse, some organizations expect any future executive to have passed through an IT management position in order to be fully equipped to hold an executive post.

IS/IT resource management and the application portfolio

Whole books have been written on the subject of the title of this chapter. In this book it is only possible to provide a broad understanding of the major issues plus some insight into critical aspects of them. Getting wrong some simple, often low level, things can cause major business problems. Two of these are discussed here before concluding on how culture and organizational aspects can be aligned to the future need to deploy IS/IT more effectively.

It is important not only to adopt a relevant management strategy in each segment of the application portfolio, but also to ensure that the right management skills are applied to the projects in the segment. As seen in Chapter 6 the driving forces, and hence requirements, in each segment differ and therefore need different management approaches or styles. The best laid plans can go awry if the individual responsible cannot deal with the types of issue that will arise. Equally, as has been said, over time an application may well move round the matrix as its role in the business changes and as the strategy for its management changes, as will the skills which are required to manage it evolve. This rationale is similar to that used in managing a product portfolio. Taking the four segments in turn as follows:

1. High potential (turnaround) applications require a style similar to wild cat products (entrepreneurial) to champion the applications through stages of uncertainty or to stop the investment if no potential exists. This implies a highly self-motivated individual who (perhaps selfishly) expects recognition of personal success but equally will not wish to be associated with failure. A risk taker, someone who does not obey the rules and in the process triggers innovation and change, is needed at this stage. Shrewd personal judgement, rather than obedience to formal management processes is most valuable. However such an individual is rarely a good team leader, nor especially committed to the organization's goals and would be dangerous on projects in other segments.

2. Strategic applications require more nurturing, to gain organizational acceptance but a clear alignment to the business objectives. A developer style of manager is required – someone who plans well, acquires and develops the necessary resources to achieve the agreed objective – seeing his or her success being dependent on demonstrating a contribution to the success of the business. An organization climber whose career in the organization is paramount, and on whose coat tails others are keen to ride, is ideal. Planning, good team management – i.e. obtaining results through others – and flexibility to changing circumstances while keeping the prime objective clearly in view are the attributes needed.

3. Factory (key operational) applications need a different style for which controller is a good term. Someone who is risk averse, who requires procedure and rules to be followed in order to ensure nothing can go wrong, is appropriate. He or she will organize resources to maximize quality control, even if speed is sacrificed. This is all relevant if such systems are not to fail due to careless change or lack of conformance to policy and procedure. Such a management style thrives in relatively stable situations and can produce stability out of turbulence by strict adherence to the rules. Clearly an entrepreneur and a controller are quite different characters.

4. Support applications require essentially a caretaker approach, managed by someone who gets satisfaction from achieving the impossible, with no resources and likes to have that skill recognized. It is a reactive, problem solving approach, getting each job

done expediently to the satisfaction of the client is more important than long-term planning. The corporate goals do not figure highly on his or her set of priorities, but ensuring small problems do not become major corporate nightmares, and hence solving them adeptly, does.

The skills of each type of manager are relevant to the different segments of the portfolio and each is equally valuable. However, if each is forced into managing in unfamiliar and alien territory, each is likely to fail. Getting the people right is just as important as getting the strategy right. In a similar way, how the IT specialists are deployed across the application portfolio will determine the long-term capability of the organization to deliver successful systems. Consider the following scenario, which is becoming increasingly common.

The existing IT professionals are bogged down in mainly the maintenance of a whole range of old factory and support systems. A new major strategic application is conceived and the internal staff cannot be released in the timescale required. The decision is taken to bring in an external organization to develop the system. The following are some of the consequences:

1. The contractor may have been given an open ended contract to meet the ever changing needs of the strategic system – almost a blank cheque.

2. No one in the IT department is capable of understanding and eventually taking responsibility for maintaining the system, nor is there any real motivation to do so.

3. The contractor has gained some very useful knowledge which might be resold to a competitor.

4. Demoralized internal staff who have been left doing the boring old work, which does not enhance their skills, often leave and in some cases join the contractor.

Thus, it can become a vicious circle, but one which can be avoided if the organization's own staff are employed on the more important strategic systems and outside resources (contractors, bureau services, facilities management, etc.) are used to deliver and maintain support and some factory systems, especially where packages can be employed. In the short term this appears unattractive but in the long term it develops the abilities of the organization, and will enable good staff to be attracted and kept. Bearing in mind the continuing shortage of skilled IT professionals this is a key aspect of IS/IT management.

Bridging the culture gap

IS/IT is a relatively new, and consequently immature, discipline in a business management context. At the same time, the technology is evolving rapidly and the management issues are forever changing. This has demanded the development of new specialists, mostly young, who see a career in IT as a primary objective and often who they work for during the development of that career as of secondary importance. Given the ever increasing demand for their skills they are very mobile. Consequently this situation can develop a major culture gap between the values of the business managers and the personal ambitions and values of the IT specialists in the organization. Meeting the business's needs is less important to the IT specialists than developing marketable skills. Into this gap, which is a yawning chasm of misunderstanding and even mistrust in many cases, many potentially important investments have fallen, having failed to deliver benefits and having incurred inordinate costs.

Somehow the gap must be bridged, while allowing for and respecting the particular needs of the people involved in a fast developing and increasingly critical business function. A number of things can be done to achieve this balance between integrating the IT function more effectively with the mainstream of the business and accommodating its special issues. Figure 8.2 attempts to depict some of the key things which organizations are doing to reduce the gulf of misunderstanding that will otherwise inhibit real progress. At the highest level the steering group provides a forum for discussing IS/IT in the business context. Developing a coherent IS/IT strategy provides a common sense of direction and commitment to a set of agreed goals and an understanding of the value IS/IT has in the business. Building the IT management positions into the management development programme, ensuring specialists can gain business management experience and vice versa, reduces the fear of the unknown and improves the overall management competence of both. At a lower level still, the development of new job roles – such as information specialists in business functions and IT specialists dedicated to providing services to a business client area – provide the means by which understanding continually develops.

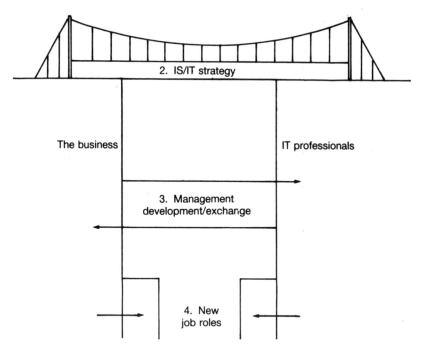

Figure 8.2 Bridging the culture gap

Perhaps all of these must be used, and many organizations are trying all four simultaneously, if the gap is to be reduced. Without at least some constructive measures being taken, nothing will change and the future will produce as many disappointments as the past and which organizations can afford that?

Summary

Not only has the IS resource to be marshalled to meet the requirements of today, but also it must be developed to meet the needs of the future. Part of that marshalling is to ensure that technical aspects of IS/IT are well managed, with an understanding of the long-term issues as well as the short-term problems of delivery of systems. Expediency today often leads to problems or poor productivity over the long term. Another part of the marshalling is bringing the total resource into alignment with the mainstream of the business and hence fitting it appropriately into the processes of the organization. As in many aspects of business, the people are ultimately the real resource, and when specialists are needed and scarce their needs must be accommodated as well as their skills deployed effectively.

While technology is becoming easier to use and manage, it is being used in a greater variety of ways, to do increasingly complex tasks. At the same time, competitive environments are becoming more intense and businesses are becoming more dependent on IS/IT for success. IS/IT skills are scarce and probably will become scarcer over the 1990s, therefore effective marshalling of the resources will become more important, not less so. This chapter has attempted to offer some guidance on how that might be achieved.

9

Social issues

In the last thirty years or so information systems' usage in organizations has grown substantially, to the point where hardly any organizations exist which do not use a computer, in fact most large organizations use many computers. During this time the application of the technology has changed substantially and this is continuing to happen. It is therefore very difficult to project how our society will be affected by the technology. Such difficulties have not stopped speculators from commenting upon the likely effects and some of these comments are to be offered here. However, be aware of the nuclear industry which in the early 1950s was projecting very low energy costs which would have had a monumental effect upon very many matters in our society. It was even said that the cost of invoicing power to the consumer would be more than the cost of generating it. Looking back, this has not been the outcome of this technology. It is possible that matters could change regarding information systems to such an extent that the future will be substantially different from that foreseen at present. Hence the comments offered below are meant to stimulate thought rather than an attempt at being definitive.

The following discussion focuses upon three issues which are the privacy of the individual, medical matters arising from usage of the technology and organizational issues and employment matters.

Some people would say that the power of the computer combined with sophisticated communications technologies provide a means by which organizations can invade the privacy of individuals. This might arise, for example, through combining income data with hobby data with inheritance data. Knowing that you are interested in flying (because you subscribe to *Popular Flying* and are a holder of a private pilots licence), combined with the knowledge of a high regular income (or at least the payment to your bank from your employer is high), combined with knowledge that you have just inherited a substantial sum may encourage a manufacturer of light aircraft to press for a sale. Some people would argue that such a method of identifying sales leads is unethical and should be prohibited by law as it invades the privacy of the person approached. Issues such as prohibiting organizations from holding information relating to an individual unless the individual has access to that information and the power to correct any inaccuracies are actively discussed. The Younger report in 1972, a government white paper in 1975, and the Lindop report in 1978 all addressed the issues of protecting the privacy of the individual. Government response to these was a white paper in 1982 which subsequently became the Data Protection Act 1984.

The Act only relates to persons of a human or corporate form controlling the processing of data automatically, thus effectively controlling the use of a computer. The Act is further restricted to personal data, i.e. that relating to living individuals. The Act is underpinned by eight principles. These are as follows:

1. Data shall be obtained and processed fairly and lawfully. Interestingly data would be deemed to be obtained unfairly if the provider was deceived or misled about the purpose for which the data were obtained. Market research data obtained by stating the use as being for one purpose yet actually using the data for a second purpose could fall foul of the Act if the data were processed on a computer subsequently.

2. Data should only be held for one or more specified and lawful purposes. The purposes need to be specified in a registration document and the usage is then limited to those purposes. This principle does not limit the processing of data, it merely requires that such activities be registered.

3. Data should not be disclosed to persons other than those described in the registration document, nor for any other purpose than that registered under the Act. Disclosure is not especially restricted; the Act merely requires that the details of such disclosures are public knowledge having being registered.

4. Data kept should be adequate, relevant and not excessive in relation to the purposes registered.

5. Data retained should be accurate and amended as circumstances change.

6. Data should only be retained for the length of time necessary for the registered purposes. When the purpose is satisfied the data should be destroyed.

7. Data should be made available to the person to whom they relate and if found to be inaccurate should be corrected.

8. Data covered by the Act should be kept secure. In particular, procedures should exist to restrict access to data; restrict alteration to data; restrict unauthorized disclosure to third parties; and prevent accidental loss of data.

If any of these principles are breached the Data Protection Registrar has the power of enforcement which may be supported by criminal sanctions. The Act may appear to be powerful and able to preserve individual privacy, yet in reality the Act effectively restricts very little. It merely means that such matters need to be registered. It is however a first step towards preserving an individual's privacy – no doubt other acts will follow.

Turning to medical issues, it is vital that these are considered at an early stage in the design of a system. For example, many word processors arrived in secretaries' offices to be located on existing desks which themselves were in a fixed environment, having lighting and such already in place. Such lack of concern for the users of the technology may be the short-term solution to a variety of issues, but time has shown that the problems do not go away. Repetitive strain injury (RSI) is a medical problem afflicting those using inappropriately sited keyboards. The height of the keyboard and the volume of usage are important issues to consider so as to avoid RSI. The incidence of RSI in some organizations is frighteningly high. Recently three computer data clerks working for the Inland Revenue were awarded £107,500 damages for RSI injuries which they developed at work. Eye-strain resulting from inadequate lighting and excessive usage of poor quality visual display unit (VDU) screens can also present significant problems. Flickering, lack of definition and inadequate brightness control can all contribute to eye strain. VDU screens emit a form of X-ray which when absorbed by humans can cause a variety of problems ranging from the minor to the loss of unborn children.

Guidelines are issued by trade unions and responsible employers and usually specify maximum amounts of time that an employee is allowed to use a screen and the minimum acceptable specification of the screens. How often such rules are observed is a matter for speculation. Some people would argue that rules for the usage of technology should be enshrined in law, whereas others argue that control should reside in the employees' hands.

Turning to employment issues, the data processing systems were first developed with efficiency as an objective. Cost benefit justifications cited reduced head count as the prime benefit. For some organizations this may have been achieved in the cited department but for many at least equal increases occurred in the data processing department. The benefits, if existing, were often obscured by other organizational changes, for example increases in volumes of transactions processed. Later systems introduced did not focus on head count reduction but rather on increased information being made available to the management and these certainly did not reduce head count.

Having said this, hopes still exist for significant reductions in the number of clerical staff required. Electronic data interchange of basic documents should reduce the rekeying of data that is prevalent with today's systems. The process of automatically capturing data at source with optical scanning and bar coding systems could have a significant impact upon the volume of keying undertaken at present. Possibly the greatest saving on the clerical front will arise from the development of organization-wide systems which should reduce the wasted effort that presently exists in reconciling information from departmentally developed systems.

There has been much speculation on the relocation of the place of work from the office to the home. Experiments have been undertaken to test the possibility of some classes of employee operating from home. Companies such as Xerox and F International have pioneered such moves. For workers with a long task cycle, requiring little interaction with other workers and a strong desire to be at home, working at home may well be suitable. Exactly how these conclusions transpose to other occupations is a matter of speculation. Some propose the development of office villages which are available for rent by an organization being located near a single worker or a group of workers. These would be fully serviced offices with the appropriate communications technologies that could be used by workers for one or two days per week. Work of the appropriate kind could be saved for this period each week. Harnessing such possibilities depend upon a worker's attributes and the nature of the task.

This issue of homeworking leads on to the future role of middle managers. Researchers hypothesize that many of today's middle managers are mostly information processors and carriers. They receive information, transform it, possibly summarize it and pass it on to the next level of management. In an organization with adequate information systems this task could be assisted greatly by the technology. Hence the conventional 'rules' of spans of control of about eight people can be amended to much higher numbers, say twenty or beyond. This change is often referred to as a flattening of the organization resulting from wider spans of control and resulting in fewer levels of management. One estimate suggests that in this way one million middle managers in the United States have been eliminated since 1979. Some take these ideas to extreme lengths and consider the total elimination of middle management. This raises the question of the future employment of long-serving middle-aged middle managers. Organizations will need to address new problems such as the source of managers for senior positions when a few middle level positions exist. Most of the views one reads are conjecture based upon very little evidence, but one thing we can be sure of is that information systems will allow organizations to support forms of organizational structure other than those commonly used today. The limits are no longer constrained by the ability to communicate.

Some speculate that our society is moving into a new era – first there was an agricultural society, followed by an industrial society, and now by an information society. It is even suggested that the great changes between the agricultural and industrial societies will be small by comparison with the coming changes. However such issues are today a matter of opinion. Some large organizations are beginning to restructure by taking advantage of information systems, but most of these changes are very much in their formative stage. Only the passing of time will allow us to know the effect of IS upon our society.

Returning to the organizational level, changes are occurring almost daily. A recent *Investors Chronicle* article recommending shares in Marks and Spencer cited the benefits accruing to them from introducing IT as the reason for purchase. Another article cited problems with IT as the reason for poor share performance. Business advantage and disadvantage resulting from IT are with us today, however the organization which neglects IT does so at its peril. We hope this book outlined the issues and the beginnings of solutions. Practitioners in IT and IS do not as yet have the answers to all the problems but be sure that the management issues in IT and IS are still developing rapidly.

Index

171

Index

172

Index

Index

Project management, 133, 148
Project plan, 122
Proprietary methods for systems
    development, 123
Prototyping, 47
    explanation of, 133
Public bodies, 55
Punched card machines, 1

Quality control systems shared, 58
Quality management, 148
    hearts and minds approach, 149

Re-engineering of information systems,
    130
Reconciliation of demand and supply, 41
Relational algebra, 127
Remedial work packages, 145
Repetitive Strain Injury (RSI), 167
Repositories in systems development, 124
Requirements analysis
    data flow diagram, 125
    project scoping, 125
Requirements analysis in systems
    development, 110, 122
Resource usage, 26
Responsibilities in systems development,
    121
Retrospective review/audit, 105
Return on investment (ROI), 88
Reuse of system components, 120
Revenue sharing, 55
Reverse engineering, 146
Review (retrospective), 105
Risk analysis, 147
Risk attaching to applications, 102
Role of IS/IT in industry, 28
Roles in systems development, 111
Routine information systems, 9

Safety critical systems, 135, 149
Sales and marketing, 62
Scarce resource, 87
Scheduling systems, links between, 58
Scoping of a project, 125
Screens, use of, 168
Security, 141
Security at the application level, 145
Security management, 145
Security requirements, specification of, 4
Security with 'ring back', 147
Senior management, 2, 4, 9, 10, 32, 33,
    34, 74
Service management, 157
Services, 62
Setting priorities for applications, 101

Share performance, 169
Shared CAD systems, 58
Shared quality control systems, 58
Shared stock planning, 59
Sharing
    examples of, 59
    of data, 14
    of systems, 14
Sharing information, 15
Sharing revenue, 55
Single page model of a business, 128
Skills, audit of, 32
Software development team, problems
    of, 143
Software engineering, 149
Software integration testing, 120
Software inventory management, 144
Span of control, 169
Specialists, 2
Speed of change in business, 28
SSADM, 124, 125
Stages in evolution of data processing, 13
Stakeholders, 33
Standard packages, 132, 136
Standards, 60
Statement of requirements, 24
Statutory Sick Pay (SSP), 132
Steering group, 41, 152, 162
Steering group executive, 155
Stifled innovation, 90
Stock control, 11
Strategic analysis, tools and techniques, 43
Strategic applications, 81
    definition of, 78
    development of, 134
Strategic decisions, 10
Strategic grid, 149 (see also Application
    portfolio)
Strategic planning process, products of, 27
Strategies for innovation, 88
Strategies, generic, 84
Strategy for main business areas, 34
Strategy implementation, 34
Strategy management
    feedback and control, 34
    formal, 33
    informal, 33
Strategy studies
    overcoming failure of, 41
    reasons for failure of, 40
Strategy, definition of, 24
Strategy, local adaptation, 34
Strengths and weaknesses (in industry), 46
Structured systems analysis, 68, 119
Supplier power, 54
Suppliers, 55

177